The Mill's Life

The Mill's Life

From the Domesday Book to the Millennium

Charles Llewellyn

with foreword and
appendix by
Roger Tabor

Robson Books

First published in Great Britain in 1997 by Robson Books Ltd,
Bolsover House, 5–6 Clipstone Street, London W1P 8LE

Foreword and appendix © 1997 Roger Tabor

British Library Cataloguing in Publication Data
A catalogue record for this title is available from the British
Library

ISBN 1 86105 105 0

Photoset in Palatino by Derek Doyle & Associates, Mold,
Flintshire. Printed and bound in Great Britain by Butler & Tanner
Ltd, London and Frome.

For those who went before
and those who have
come after

Foreword by Roger Tabor

My girlfriend had noticed an advertisement in the paper about a mill for sale. 'Oh yes,' I had said with my mind on other things. Later we drove past it by chance and I stopped the car to look at this wonderful building.

'It's the one that's for sale,' she reminded me.

'Oh,' I said. It was love at first sight and I began negotiations.

That was how I met Charles Llewellyn, whose boyhood home was the Mill house alongside, and for whom the Mill had always been 'part of his life'. In selling the Mill to me he dramatically changed my life into being a mill owner and all that goes with it (which can include raising the sluice at three o'clock in the morning, with a storm raging and the river rising). However, it turned out not to be a simple transaction for the Mill was full of dust and dead starlings, but Charles came to my rescue by allowing me to live at the Mill house as work proceeded.

As a naturalist and social historian I was drawn to the Mill and its landscape, but as a TV presenter and producer I suppose it was inevitable that I would make a TV series about a place that is unique yet has a wider story of past times. Consequently I made and presented the BBC television series *The Mill's Life* with Bowe Tennant Productions over a three year period, looking at the evolving story of the Mill from its beginnings until today. Due to my previous TV series and books on cats of course my present day mill cats featured incidentally, but so too did previous generations of mill cats. Charles, who turned out to be a natural raconteur on camera, fondly reminisced about the Siamese cat of his youth who had its broken leg set in plaster by the surgeon at the local hospital.

Within the story that I told in the TV series Charles and his family were a point of significant transition, because his father installed his family in the Mill house as the Mill finished its working life, yet the water was still used for power. Charles is a direct contact with a way of life that has slipped away. His own childhood as recalled in both this book and the series was in an idyllic setting of English country house living encompassed by the waterways of the Mill.

In the series I then followed the story to see how a new set of inhabitants of the Mill house, Mill, granary and connected buildings settled in to live with the past. This book looks at that same story from a very different and amusing perspective. The book was written independently of the series, and is quite different in approach, but as they both look at the same subjects they make good companions. For those who would like to remember aspects of the series in the context of Charles' narrative I have penned an appendix that readers can find at the end of the book.

Charles' story is one told with fond recollection and good humour – although the latter is often at my expense! This is the side of the story not told in the TV series, of the mud and mayhem and often hilarious outcomes, that emerged from the very English concern of feeling a responsibility for old buildings.

Chapter One

My father died in July 1990 in the middle of the worst property slump since the Second World War. His legacy to his three children and eight grandchildren was a modest portfolio of stocks and shares, accumulated haphazardly over the years, and Fulford Mill.

He had been a successful barrister for 30 years and then a county court judge. He had bought Fulford Mill in 1947, when property prices were low after the war and the pressure of living in a small, three-bedroomed house on the outskirts of Banktree, with three young children and a nanny, had proved too exhausting for his limited patience. So, at the age of two, I was moved with my two older sisters and a broken arm to the rambling six-bedroomed, part-Georgian, part-Elizabethan Mill house standing in 25 acres, on a country lane straddling the parish boundary between the villages of Black Nutleam and Crossing in the north of Essex.

On the other side of the lane, a five-storey water mill, dating from the eighteenth century, towered over the front garden of the house. Next to it, across an open area of hard standing used as our car park, was a granary from the same period. Stretching up the lane and abutting the Elizabethan section of the house was a long range of outbuildings, known as the stable yard and cart lodge and past that, round a sharp bend in the lane at the top of the garden, was a cottage, once used by workers on the estate.

The River Blackwater flowed through the Mill and through a tunnel under the front garden of the house, opening into a tail water, which flowed down beside a 70-yard-long path, lined on both sides with hazel trees, to the bottom of the garden. The Mill itself had a sluice gate, which could be opened after rain, so that the head of water could gush through another tunnel under the lane into a mill pool and then meander down its natural course to join the tail water at the end of the garden.

Between these two stretches of the river an earlier owner had planted a shrubbery of ornamental plants among the yew and holly trees.

I sat in my father's clean, modern, 12 by 14 room in the nursing home in Long Melford on a warm July day in 1990. My father lay, small and huddled on the bed, hyperventilating and unconscious, wheezing out the last hours of his 82-year life, surrounded by a few possessions from his home, a watercolour of Fulford Mill, his walking stick, a photograph of my mother sitting on the dwarf wall outside the dining-room window with Henry, their black Labrador, and another of my oldest sister Anne and her husband Peter in Southern Rhodesia, as it had then been. His tatty, brown, woollen jacket with the leather patches on the elbows hung over the back of a green, plastic armchair.

Depressed by the incongruity of his surroundings and distressed by the symptoms of his departure, I kissed his bristly face with its rodent ulcers of skin cancer, for the last time in life and went out into the long, main street of the old Suffolk town.

I wandered slowly along the antique shops in the warm, summer sun, letting the memories of childhood in this corner of East Anglia flood through my mind. The café in the High Street, where Douglas Hale and I had so often revived ourselves with greasy eggs, bacon and fried bread after some nocturnal, teenage jaunt, now an antique shop selling Regency furniture; the sharp bend at the end of the straight stretch, where I had so nearly met an early demise on one high-speed journey home from Cambridge, now turned into a roundabout by a solicitous local council.

After the well-attended funeral in the small Norman church in Crossing, I sat by the Aga in the kitchen at Fulford Mill, the garish, orange wallpaper a testimony to my mother's individual sense of interior design, drinking tea with my two sisters, Anne and Juliet, and Anne's husband Peter, and wondered where to begin in disposing, not so much of the furniture, which was crammed into every room, giving the house all the elegance and co-ordination of a Pickford's warehouse, but of the voluminous clutter which our parents had amassed over 43 years of love, marriage, divorce (ours not theirs), children, grandchildren, bereavement, inheritance, friends, family and employees. It seemed to fill every room, every cupboard, every shelf, and every available spare surface in the large, lugubrious old house. The wooden skis and luges which were a memory of my father's brief school period in Vevey on Lake Geneva in 1924, the antique golf clubs in the brown canvas bag last used when Queen Victoria was on the throne, ancient typewriters and sewing machines, cupboards filled with shoes, old wine boxes filled with files and others with learned law journals, drawers full of wool, knitting needles, pieces of material, patterns, boxes of children's games with pieces missing, a leather suitcase containing the regalia of my father's Freemasonry, empty gilt picture frames, early radios and box cameras, metal steam trains and model aircraft, fishing rods, tea chests of paper-wrapped crockery and glass. Everywhere there were boxes and trunks with a fine, or not so fine, layer of dust and the filigree of spiders' webs and everywhere there were books and then more books. They started in neat order in the many bookcases and shelves and then spilled on to the floor. They stood in an untidy pile behind my mother's armchair by the fireplace in the living-room; they lined the floor of the upstairs landing leading to the door of our nanny, Lucy's, bedroom. They hid behind old, brown, velvet curtains on the deep shelf in the aptly named 'junk hole'; they filled the lead-lined butler's sink beneath the food counter in the big larder; they lay spilling out of trunks and moulding on the floor in the Granary. The complete works of Thackeray stood among dusters and tins of polish on the shelf in the scullery cupboard.

The five garages were the same. Apart from my parents' Honda and Austin mini, they contained dilapidated lawn-mowers, our old bicycles, bundles of oak paling which my father had guarded jealously, piles of furniture, kitchen chairs and tables, disused engines, empty cans of petrol and oil, leather harnesses and nosebags for carthorses, a large metal vat, used for whitewashing the lines on the grass tennis court and another for carting water to the pasture meadows, redundant washing machines, cookers and boilers, and suitcases covered with the labels of earlier journeys and filled with clothes.

My parents never threw anything away and they were both only children, so that when their respective parents had died the contents of their houses had been stored at Fulford Mill 'for future use'. The garages contained the mute history of three generations of our family.

The stables were no different. Among the metal cornbins and piles of firewood stood ancient garden implements with broken handles, piles of clay, flower pots, sack barrows with small metal wheels and wooden shafts, boxes filled with hammers, chisels, wedges and unidentifiable lumps of metal covered with grease, bundles of wooden fencing stakes and old black paraffin heaters. The mangers were filled with rolls of chicken wire and empty paint tins with pieces of wood, with which some earlier handyman had stirred the paint, now frozen immobile in the solid remnants at the bottom; from wooden pegs on the walls hung dried flowers, harnesses, wooden scythes, bill hooks, baling twine and an old, brown, leather jerkin.

Anne was brisk and businesslike as usual. She sat beautifully upright on the hard kitchen chair, a legacy of years of my father instructing her 'Don't hunch', the neon, kitchen light reflected off her glasses:

'We'll divide up the furniture that's worth having and sell the rest. Then Charlie can burn the rubbish that's left over before we sell the house.'

I smiled at the simple operation that she envisaged from the security and distance of her well-ordered house in Dublin. I suspected even at this early stage that this was something which was going to consume several years of my life.

As my father's executor and the only one of his children still resident in England, I knew that the main onus of winding up his affairs was going to fall on me. I had observed his efforts at attempting to wind up the estate of my wealthy and eccentric Great Uncle Walter, which had finally ended after seven years of confusion, bickering, legal argument and compromise with a legacy which, in my case, as one of his beneficiaries, had been sufficient to pay for some urgent repairs to the Horsham slab roof of my house in Surrey. Since it was a listed building at least English Heritage would have appreciated my father's efforts.

Juliet, the younger of my older sisters by two years, was considerate as always. She leaned forward on her forearms on the kitchen table in a characteristic gesture with an expression of concern in her hazel eyes.

'It's going to be a big job for Charlie on his own. At least we could sort out all the clothes, china and linen and things like that in the house on this trip. We might even have time to clear the house.'

Everything to my sisters was a 'trip'. Juliet had travelled from her home in Canada for the funeral and time was crucial to her, before she had to return to work, organizing functions for the Canadian Egg Marketing Board. Anne agreed at once:

'That's a good idea,' emphasizing 'that'. 'Let's get started. Where are the dusters?'

They went out into the passage to reconnoitre the enemy territory, their dark heads bobbing up and down in communication as they chattered. I had a momentary feeling of concern for the fat spiders, lurking undisturbed for so many years behind the free-standing wardrobes in the beamed back bedrooms, at the impending disruption to their tranquil lives. I needn't have worried.

I leaned back in the wooden, farmhouse chair cradling my cup of tea and gazed bleakly at Peter, one of life's delights. A calm, gentle and intelligent accountant approaching retirement from his career with the Investment Bank of Ireland, always alert to and considerate of other people's feelings. He smiled helpfully:

'We'll give you all the help we can, Charlie.' His eyes twinkled. I smiled back as cheerfully as I could. Inside, I felt like a sandcastle on the beach with a tidal wave lurking offshore.

I was in the property business, or more precisely, had been in the property business. Not that I started there. After three years studying bridge, football and the guitar, I had left Cambridge with a degree in Economics and had worked briefly in New York for a company importing fine bone china and English silver, until the authorities indicated, in a long, manila envelope, postmarked Washington DC, that they wished to enlist me in the US Army. Having no appetite for military adventures in the dangerous jungle of Vietnam, I left my job, took a hurried and rather nail-biting holiday on a Greyhound bus to California and caught a TWA flight to Heathrow. Back in England I enlisted instead in the somewhat safer film production industry and, at the age of 22, joined John Harrod and Partners, a company specializing in the production of television commercials.

There followed four years of fun and excitement in the London of Mary Quant, Biba, Terence Conran and the Rolling Stones.

Commercial television was in its infancy and John Harrod and Partners was one of the hottest companies in the industry. We had a roster of famous feature film directors under contract for commercials and the advertising agencies which were our clients were anxious to employ their skills. No one seemed to know what commercials ought to cost and, as a result, money was no object, provided the client liked the finished product. Since he had no historical precedent against which to make a judgement, it was a brave client who expressed himself dissatisfied.

I had been making amateur films as a hobby from the age of 16 and I was now able to indulge my interest at somebody else's expense. Samuel Goldwyn described film-making as 'playing with the biggest train set in the world' and for me it certainly was not like having a proper job. I threw myself into my role as producer with all the energy and enthusiasm of youth.

The hours were long but the rewards were great. Not only was there the satisfaction of translating ideas into film, but as advertising budgets grew and agencies became more adventurous, foreign locations became ever more popular as the settings for our mini-masterpieces. In addition, no one cared how you dressed or what you looked like. Coming from the background of my father's sombre dark suits, his highly polished shoes and the wigs and robes of his profession, this was a welcome relief.

I reverted from the business suits of my period in New York to the black leather jacket and faded Levi jeans of my university years and thence progressed to the flowered shirts and flared velvet trousers that emanated from the flower-power era in San Francisco. My hair, I had a lot then, grew ever longer. John Harrod, the owner of the company and its chairman, a tall, fair-haired man with white eyebrows, an urbane manner and an acute commercial sense, smiled indulgently at the chameleon-like performance of his latest recruit, 'You look like a hippy, Charles.'

Since most of the writers and art directors who were his principal source of business looked more like hippies than I did, I took this as a compliment. I grew a Zapata moustache and took to smoking Havana cigars to complete my film producer's outfit. Thus disguised from my former Cambridge peer group in their Procter & Gamble uniforms, I travelled the world, filming commercials in exotic foreign locations.

During the course of this unexpected life, I married my girlfriend, Nova, a tall blonde model from Norwich, who was attempting to establish a career in acting, and moved from my third-floor flat in Baker Street over a travel agency and a small solicitors' practice to a terraced house in Fulham, sandwiched between Bert, a friendly jeweller from the North End Road and Alf, a widowed stoker from Battersea power station, who lived entirely on cheese and Guinness.

In 1970, John Harrod rewarded my single-handed efforts to turn the London commercial production industry into Hollywood and surprisingly appointed me as managing director of the company. I sat in the shiny, sand-coloured Alfa Romeo, which came with the promotion, outside the company's offices, an elegant red-brick building in a leafy mews street in Mayfair, at the age of 26 and thought, 'This is God's own job.'

In fact, the promotion distanced me from my love of film-making and introduced me to the more mundane business of running a profitable company and making money. So it was, that in 1971, I rewarded John Harrod's faith in me, by abruptly resigning and, with the arrogance of my years, forsaking God's job for one of my own, by forming my own production company with Tom Bussmann, a tall, second-generation, Jewish immigrant from Berlin, with shoulder-length, dark hair and an evil sense of humour, who was one of the film directors at Harrods.

I returned home to Fulham a week after the birth of our son Talfryn. Nova was entertaining an old friend to tea. Jean looked at me as I came in:

'Hello, Charles, Nova tells me you're very successful.'

'Actually, I'm unemployed. I've just resigned.'

Nova was standing by the door with the baby in her arms. It was one of the few times I ever saw her speechless.

Tom's sense of humour was more original than Mel Brooks, Woody Allen and Lenny Bruce rolled into one. He was a walking Sid Caesar show and we coined the company slogan 'Work with Bussmann, Llewellyn for a laugh'. It paid dividends. Enough clients arrived in our offices in Soho for us to laugh all the way to the National Westminster so that, at the end of the first full year, I was wondering how to invest the surplus profits. Since by this time I had sold the house in Fulham for three times what I had paid for it only two years before and moved to a suburban villa in East Sheen, I decided to diversify my risk away from the profitable but precarious film business into bricks and mortar, and started a property company.

The next 15 years passed in something of a blur. The film and property companies both prospered. As managing director of both, I worked long hours. Our daughter Celina was born two months prematurely in 1973. I visited her each evening after work in the premature baby unit in Charing Cross Hospital and held her tiny hand through the hole in the incubator. Her forefinger was the length of my nail. Nova's career as an actress progressed in fits and starts much to her frustration. We moved house frequently, partly as a result of Nova's restlessness and partly as a consequence of the rising property prices of that time. In 1976 Nova managed to secure a role in a long-running West End play, *No Sex Please, We're British*. Unfortunately, ignoring the title she decided to trade me in for a younger model. Divorce followed.

I didn't take this as badly as I should have done and after a brief period camping out in the spare bedroom of my producer Jo Godman and her husband Keith, I moved down to Fulford Mill for a few weeks while I negotiated to purchase the statutory tenancy of one of the property company's unconverted flats in Hurlingham Gardens in Fulham.

The tenant, Mr Ramanathan, a technician from the local hospital, stood before me, his brown eyes and plump cheeks beaming broadly beneath his thick black hair.

'Ooh yes, this is indeed fortunate,' he said. 'For years I have been wanting to return to India to join the Save the Tiger Campaign. It is a lifelong ambition of mine and it is only the lack of funds which have prevented me.'

His wife stood silently beside him. I sensed that she did not entirely share his interest in tigers.

'With the money you are paying me to leave, I can fulfil my ambition.'

In a moment of generosity, he insisted that I accept the gift of his folding double bed. I noticed that it only had three legs, the fourth corner being supported by a pile of old copies of the *British Medical Journal*. I accepted his gift graciously and our negotiations were concluded.

I learned later that he used the money which I had paid him to rehouse his wife into a flat in Fulham Palace Road, while he moved into a flat in Battersea with a nurse from St Bartholomew's Hospital. With a feeling of guilt, I sent a donation to the Save the Tiger Campaign.

I set about converting the flat by calling in James Deacon, a Fulham builder on the verge of bankruptcy, who viewed the job much as one might view a distant relative in an old people's home: something to be thought about often, but visited only rarely.

Living in a building site seemed to suit me and I continued with my long working hours, unfettered by the need for the consideration of family. At the home of an old rugby-playing friend, I met Annette, a tall and attractive blonde, who cooked directors' lunches for Barclays Bank. We shared long, happy walks through the beautiful Surrey hills and Annette cooked succulent meals to last me through the week in London. After a while, she came to live in my building site with her calm, blue eyes and excitable Red Setter and on a hot July day we were married in Chelsea Register Office.

Annette did not approve of the fact that I slept in a second-hand, three-legged bed, nor of the fact that in her first winter in occupation, the only way to keep warm, in the absence of conventional heating, was to lie together in the enormous, cast-iron bath with the diminishing hot water emanating from the shower rose held up by our shoulders. Personally, I thought it was the most enjoyable heating system yet to be invented.

A year later on another July day, Annette woke me when I had selfishly overslept and calmly announced that her contractions were coming every five minutes. I battled, panic-stricken through the stationary, rush-hour traffic on the Embankment and we arrived at St Thomas's Hospital just before our daughter Juliet.

Spurred by this addition to our family, we began to look in earnest for a house in the country and on one dismal December day in 1982, we helped the removal men carry our furniture into a run-down, fifteenth-century farmhouse in Surrey, surrounded by farm buildings and seven acres of land. I thought at the time of the similarity of its name, age, position and layout to Fulford Mill and wondered why we hadn't moved into a house called 'The Willows' or 17 Acacia Avenue.

Annette's younger brother Bill was a qualified carpenter, currently unemployed and living with his mother in Plymouth. At Annette's suggestion, I telephoned him. I explained that we had moved into a dilapidated house in Surrey and if he didn't have anything better to do, we could give him three or four months' work getting it straight. This December I bought him a fishing rod to commemorate ten years' careful and meticulous work on the house.

Annette exchanged one building site for another and I exchanged London life for the pleasures of commuting. Our respective projects became bigger. Annette calmly masterminded the conversion of the house, cooked meals for the family on a primus stove on her knees in the hallway, with a baby at her breast and happily gave birth to Edward in Mount Alvernia Hospital in Guildford, having taken the precaution of going in early to avoid my unreliable transport arrangements. I bought a large warehouse in Richmond and turned it into 50 serviced offices.

I was spending more and more time on the property company. The film company was flourishing, without much input from me, under Tom's able and creative hand. I bought an industrial property company from a benign 70-year-old from the East End, with offices in St James's, and worked even longer hours. Fortunately, outside agencies rescued me from this anti-social routine and probably a second divorce, when Tom bought my shares in the film company and a large public company purchased the property company and appointed me to their board. For two years the pressure diminished, even if the hours did not, until the public company was itself taken over in the raging bull market of the late eighties and I was cut free with a lump sum in compensation and a capital-gains-tax problem.

The bald-headed young whizz-kid, who had masterminded the acquisition of our company, smiled wolfishly at us across the boardroom table, as we signed our contract release forms and received our compensation cheques:

'Well, gentlemen, perhaps you should take Rousseau's advice and go and cultivate your gardens.'

'Voltaire,' I muttered, *sotto voce*, little knowing how prophetic his words were to prove to be.

Providence had made me uniquely suited to organize the disposal of a large, rambling mill house and estate in Essex in 1990. I was available, with no undue pressure to seek immediate employment, I knew the place intimately, I had a working life's experience of residential property and the M25 made the journey from Surrey to north Essex bearable.

Chapter Two

David Forrest, the partner from Strutt & Parker, was a dark-haired young man with a relaxed professional style and a Daks tweed jacket. He was cautious:

'Of course, the market's down, but it's a character house and they are much sought after.'

'Should we sell it as one lot or break it up into different lots?'

'Well, some people might see the Mill and outbuildings as a liability, but we do get a lot of inquiries for small estates.'

'Should I modernize it to make it appear less . . .' I hunted for the right word, 'decrepit?'

I could hear my father turning in his grave. He abhorred change of any sort and if he could have heard me describing Fulford Mill as 'decrepit' he would have been outraged. He had not responded positively to my gentle remark 30 years before that the wallpaper in the hall was 40 years old and it might be nice to think of redecorating, nor my observation that the bathroom was located in a corridor, down two steps from the landing and up another, leading into another landing which contained the door to my bedroom.

This curious arrangement meant that when I wanted to go to bed, I had to hover downstairs with one ear open for the sound of the metal catch to the bathroom door and, when I heard the occupant leaving by the creak of the loose floorboard on the landing, make a singleminded dash for my room, like a grey-hound from the trap. Once there, I had to undress quickly and get back into the bathroom, before one of my sisters comman-deered the bath for an inordinate period, waiting for the water to heat up again, due to the tank being several sizes too small for a house with six occupants.

Frequently I fell asleep, unwashed and with unbrushed teeth, and awoke at two o'clock in the morning with the bathroom enticingly empty, but too sleepy to enjoy it.

To my father, however, coming from an age that had wit-nessed the advent of modern plumbing, such an arrangement was acceptable, if not luxurious. Since the family held back out of deference for him to have the first bath, he was not aware of the jostling for position that occurred after he had retired. He greeted my suggestion that the small boxroom at the back of the second landing would make an ideal and self-contained bath-room: with a frosty stare!

'It would cost a lot of money.'

He considered money spent on the house to be wasted.

'It would be very simple,' I countered, 'the outside plumbing is in the right position and I could move the bath and sink myself.'

'You don't know anything about building,' he said with final-ity. It was useless. To him, a house was to be lived in exactly as you found it. If something went wrong or was an inconvenience, you mended the symptom and ignored the cause, or else you simply lived with it. I christened this disease Millitis.

I had selected Strutt & Parker to handle the sale of the house solely because my father had wished it. The young man consid-ered my remark.

'Well, a lot of people like an unmodernized house,' he ven-tured. I understood why my father had chosen his firm. They were made for each other. I had a brief mental picture of the dozens of houses in London, which I had converted and sold at a handsome profit, but concluded that the young man would probably consider that I didn't know anything about building.

Finally, it was decided that he would go away and prepare a sales brochure, incorporating some photographs showing the house and grounds in their best light and that we would start a marketing campaign offering the estate 'as a whole or in lots'. In the meantime we would look for a tenant, so that at least the house would be occupied and looked after, while we were waiting for offers.

After a few weeks, I was summoned down to meet some prospective tenants. Mr and Mrs Green were a friendly couple in late middle age. Recently retired and returned from Canada they were willing to take the house on a monthly, furnished tenancy.

They were ideal tenants and the arrangement suited me well. I was able to leave most of the furniture in the house, while my two sisters and myself decided who should have what, and arrangements could be made for shipments in due course to Ireland and Canada. I was also able to visit the house from time to time and start nibbling away at the gargantuan task of sifting the contents.

I decided to start this process by sorting out everything that could clearly be identified as 'rubbish'. With this in mind, I ventured up to the stable yard with the intention of starting a pile of metal objects, which could have no further use, but which could be carted away by a totter. I went in to the first stable and on one of the old metal cornbins I met my first challenge. It was a fist-sized lump of metal with a circular hole through the centre and irregular, square grooves in the sides. I picked it up and remembered asking Bearman what it was, 30 years earlier.

Bearman was my parents' full-time gardener and odd-job man. A short, stout, bald man of indeterminate age, he had been inherited by my parents from their predecessor, Francis Blyth, who had been the last person to run the Mill as a business from 1914 to 1947. Bearman had worked in the Mill until my parents bought it and then had graduated to general handyman of the house and grounds. He was a gentle, placid, uncomplaining man with a notable Essex accent. He'd picked up the piece of metal, 'Tha' Charles,' he said, 'tha' be a sprigget.'

'What's that?' I asked, 'what's a sprigget?'

'How d'ya mean?'

'Well, what's a sprigget? What's it for?'

'It's mechanical,' he said, as if this was an explanation.

Further questions failed to elicit more detailed information. I looked at the piece of metal again. Was it rubbish? That was my criterion now. What *was* a sprigget? I remembered having looked the word up in the *Shorter Oxford English Dictionary* 30 years before and not having found it. Did Bearman know what a sprigget was or had he made the word up to conceal his ignorance? There were many words in his vocabulary which did not feature in the textbooks. Was there a demand for spriggets now? Would we need a sprigget in some mechanical emergency in the Mill?

Depressed at my inability to determine whether the first thing I'd picked up was rubbish or not, I put it in my pocket thinking it would make an intriguing paperweight for my desk at home and went back into the house. Mrs Green cheerfully gave me a gin and tonic and I stood looking out of the bay window in the living-room listening to her chatting on about her life in Canada and wondering how many more 'spriggets' I would find.

Feeling revived by the gin and tonic, I decided to continue my efforts indoors. I went down the passage to the long, low room in the Elizabethan part of the house, with two windows looking out on to the lane. As children, this had been two small rooms, the back one being used for food storage and the front one as a playroom.

As teenagers, the front room had been made over to us three children and the back room, with its concrete floor, had fallen into disuse. One evening, when my father was away in London, I began idly to pick at the wall between the two rooms to see if it would be possible to take it down and make one larger room, which we urgently needed. My mother came into the room and stood behind me.

'Your father won't be happy with you doing that,' she smiled.

'I'm just seeing what the wall's made of.'

She picked up a chisel and poked tentatively at the wall herself.

'It's lath and plaster.'

'We could take it down and make one larger room. It would be much better.'

'Yes it probably would.'

We attacked the wall together. Under our combined efforts in little more than an hour, we had one large room and were standing ankle deep in debris, observing the fine old oak beam, which we had exposed. My mother smiled in approval at our efforts. I think she enjoyed her moment of rebellion against my father's resistance to change.

My father was shocked and indignant on his return from work. 'Hrmph,' he hrmphed, standing in the passage by the open door in his bowler hat and dark overcoat, carrying his attaché case and furled umbrella. I called it his bailiff's outfit. 'I suppose this is your doing?'

My mother seemed to have disappeared. Standing there with a club hammer in my hand and covered in plaster dust it was difficult to deny, but during his absences at work over the next few weeks, my mother, Bearman and myself set about restoring the room. Bearman hacked off the plaster to the damp, exterior wall and formed a dampproof course from red plastic fertilizer bags. My mother bought more orange wallpaper and together we painted and papered the room. Finally, we laid a grey fitted carpet. My father grudgingly acknowledged our efforts and after we three children had left home, he moved his desk, books and papers into it and it became his study.

I sat down in the small, round-backed chair at his Georgian mahogany bureau and pulled out one of the long drawers. It was crammed to overflowing with letters in blue Basildon Bond envelopes, addressed in a flamboyant, feminine hand and post-marked Crowborough. I knew they came from my elderly, maiden Great Aunt Elsie. My father had been her only living relative and they had corresponded once a week for 20 years, to my knowledge. I took one letter out of its envelope and read it. It was dated 1959.

My darling Jack,

We are having terrible weather here. Quite a gale. I do so hope that you are not having the same. The people here are really quite nice and I know they do try their best, but it just isn't the same as the last place. I do find that I miss Miss Piper and I don't know what I'd do without your letters. You are so good to me.

Only a short letter this time, darling boy.

Your affectionate

Elsie

I opened another, dated July 1968.

My darling Jack,

It is unbearably hot here. I hope it is a little bit cooler where you are. Miss Piper used to simply hate the heat. The people here have been very nice to me. We sat in the garden yesterday and had tea. I am looking forward so much to your visit next weekend. I don't know what I'd do without you, darling boy.

Your affectionate

Elsie

I counted the letters. There were 470 of them. I selected three at random and hesitantly dropped the rest into a plastic bin-liner, then I drove back to Surrey, attempting to redefine the word 'rubbish'.

From August 1990 to December, with the country in recession and the property market in the doldrums, we had no positive response to our marketing campaign. I decided to take the house off the market for a while. The Greens continued happily with their monthly tenancy and I made frequent trips from Surrey to continue with the process of clearing the house. It seemed to have no effect. I became more ruthless in my definition of rubbish, but no matter how much I burnt, or how many trips I made to the council tip in Albaton with my wife's Volvo Estate crammed with rusting lumps of metal, just as much seemed to remain. Clearing the Augean stables was a little light housework compared to clearing Fulford Mill.

I decided that I must at least clear my father's papers and sat down once more at his desk, sifting through drawers of correspondence, boxes of programmes for shows and autographed menus of ceremonial dinners, going back to 1936.

There were letters from a wide range of people, from pupils and solicitors, from grateful and not-so-grateful clients, from distant cousins, local tradesmen and the Crossing vicar, from his Freemason's Lodge, the Inner Temple and the Law Society and from his clubs, Boodles and the Athenaeum. I skimmed through many of them and was fascinated by the views that the writers had of my father.

From the viewpoint of his three children, our father was someone to be avoided at all costs. With his sharp, legal mind he was endlessly argumentative and opinionated. It was as if, having spent the week in court, being paid to stand up and argue, he was unable to drop the habit when he returned at the weekend to the casual jumble that was family life at Fulford Mill.

In the early years of my awareness of this critical and disputatious nature, my mother used to give as good as she got, since it was normally she who bore the brunt of his sarcasm or intervened on our behalf if one of us children was the target for his barbed comments. She had a quick brain and was able to express herself with what I found to be a pleasing simplicity, which only served to infuriate my father further. However, being of a more easy-going nature or perhaps just being wiser, over the years she gradually rose to the bait less and less until, after many years of verbal manoeuvring around each other, they arrived at a mutual truce, in which my father's tortuous, but syntactically correct and beautifully polished, three-minute harangues would be greeted by my mother saying quietly after a moment's pause, 'What did you say dear, I'm just trying to sew these name tags on?'

It was as if they had fought themselves to an honourable draw. However, during their argumentative period there were some classics. I remember one Sunday lunchtime my father complained about the toughness of the roast beef and criticized my mother's choice of butcher adding, for good measure, a dissertation on the merits of every butcher within a five-mile radius, about which, to my certain knowledge, he knew nothing. My mother was furious and responded with a tirade of her own, to the effect that she had been using Lay's the butcher ever since they had moved into their first home in York Gardens and before any of us children were born; that my father knew that and had never complained before and if he didn't like it he could do the shopping himself in future.

The atmosphere crackled. We three children beat a hasty retreat to the safety of the bedroom above the kitchen at the top of the stairs, which my sisters shared. We closed the door and stood looking at each other in shocked silence. Anne clenched and unclenched her fists in a gesture of impotent indignation. Juliet was close to tears. It seemed mildly funny to me.

There was silence as my father digested my mother's response and she began wheeling the trolley, laden with the lunch plates, through the hallway from the dining-room to the kitchen. Then he followed her into the hall and opened a second front on the subject of the housekeeping budget. I inched the door open in order to be able to hear his continued diatribe. A frosty silence emanated from the kitchen. My father stalked back into the dining-room. A minute or two later my mother came back into the hallway carrying a tray of coffee cups and saying in a loud voice, 'Mrs Beeton couldn't cater for a man as fussy as you,' as she went into the living-room, on the opposite side of the hall from the dining-room.

Boldly, I crept out of my sisters' bedroom and went up the five stairs opposite to the landing above the hallway, waiting for my father's response. Nervously Anne and Juliet joined me and we knelt breathlessly on the landing with our ears pressed to the banister rails, as the battle raged beneath us.

It was all so mannered. Having been brought up in an age when divorce was unheard of and throwing plates was considered *infra dig*, the only battlefield left to my parents was verbal. There they sat in two different rooms unable to see each other, hurling insults across the intervening hall, like rival artillery batteries throwing shells across No Man's Land, while upstairs we three children, the poor bloody infantry, commented on their performances and made suggestions:

'Ooh, he shouldn't have said that.'

'She should have said he left the stable door open and Rom got out.'

'Well, I didn't think the beef was any good either.'

I began to giggle. The row continued spasmodically most of the afternoon until teatime, but by then I had remembered my bicycle waiting in the wash house and was halfway to the ford at Bradwell with my jam jar to catch sticklebacks, wondering where Mrs Beeton lived.

Remembering how difficult our father had been in the early years of our childhood, I was surprised to read in the bundles of correspondence how affectionately he had been regarded by others. There was a short letter, scrawled on a piece of lined paper from a Mr Evans of HM Prison, Chelmsford. My father had defended him unsuccessfully and he had been sent down for two years for burglary. He seemed more concerned about the blow to my father's professional pride than his forthcoming period of enforced inactivity:

Dear Mr Llewellyn,

You did your best. You got up there and put my case as well as anyone could. I never thought I had much of a chance and you did well to get me only two years. I liked that bit about my being a married man. I may be married, but I haven't seen Margaret for three years now.

Yours respectfully,

David Evans

There was a letter from Denis Parsons, who owned the garage on the outskirts of Banktree where my parents had an account, thanking my father for the loan of a thousand pounds when his business was in danger of going into liquidation. Denis with his mechanical genius and Dr Kildare looks became a good friend of my own when, in my late teens and having passed my driving test, I went to him with a succession of beaten up old bangers, in order for him to help me keep them on the road and within the bounds of the law, but neither he nor my father ever mentioned the loan.

There were letters from his old school, St Christopher's at Letchworth, thanking him for presenting the prizes at speechday and from the Emmanuel College Law Society for speaking at their annual dinner. There were letters from many firms of solicitors thanking him for the successful or unsuccessful outcomes of their mutual cases, all expressed as to a friend rather than a professional.

There were several letters from Mrs Baker, who lived at the top of Fulford Lane, thanking him for trying to get one of her sons a job at Lake and Elliotts.

It was as if my father were two different people, keeping his stern side for his family and his more human one for outsiders. Either that or he edited his correspondence carefully.

There were letters addressed to my mother too, one in particular, neatly folded and headed 92, East Street, Banktree, was a letter of resignation from Lucy Downham our nanny or, as she liked to call herself, our maid:

Dear Madam,
    I cannot tell you how very sorry I am about things. I'm not trying to excuse myself, but I know that I've been letting myself get into a nervy state of mind and ever since Easter, things have seemed so much worse. Perhaps after all they were not as bad as I thought and things that I thought so much against me were not so. I am truly sorry and I do hope that you will soon get a really nice maid without a temper. You have been so kind and considerate and I heartily wish that I had told you quietly that I didn't feel fit (especially Swanage).
    Goodbye and thank you very much for all your kindness.
    Yours respectfully
                    Lucy Downham

It was dated 1946. Since Lucy remained in my parents'
employment until her death in 1976, first as nanny, then as cook,
housekeeper, friend and confidante, I could only assume that the
upset implicit in her letter had been overcome by my mother's
normal tact and good humour.

My mind went back to the times she had taken us three children on blackberry-picking walks. We would ramble along the
river through the long, thin pasture meadow in the late summer
sun, as far as the narrow footbridge by Bluebell Wood. There
were more fish in the river then and it was not unusual to see the
bright blue flash of the pair of kingfishers who made that stretch
of river their haunt. We would turn round at the footbridge and
walk back along the hedge, watching the rabbits playing around
the massive fallen trunk of a majestic oak, turned white with the
sun of countless summers, filling our wicker baskets with black-
berries, while Lucy told us stories of her childhood in the East
End.

There was a letter to my mother from No B54136 Peter Hines,
addressed from HM Prison, Jebbs Avenue, Brixton, SW2 dated
14 May 1982:

Dear Rae,

I hope letters are getting out of here OK. This one is to
say how much I'm missing my cucumber sandwiches and
to ask if you'd pass on messages to a few people, please, as
they haven't let me have my address book.

1 To Charles and Annette and new baby, when he or she
arrives. Please tell Charles that I'll never forget how he
drove down to see me from London seven years ago. Ask
him if he remembers the tandem and riding over to New
Hall on it, or when he stopped Robbie Gordon from
thumping me in the coffee bar for looking at his girlfriend. He might be amused to hear that after 20 years of
warning from my Ma that someone would hit me on the
nose if I didn't keep my mouth shut - eventually on
Wednesday in a cell waiting to go on at Bow Street - it
happened. I forgot that one of my fellow inmates was six

foot wide and in there for armed robbery, I swore at him and he punched me in the mouth - nice people I meet.

2 To my godson Talfryn. Please tell him that his godfather is neither bad nor mad and that I had a royal wedding crown for him for months, but eventually used it to buy some flowers for Mrs Thatcher the day before I was arrested! What a bloody awful waste of money - and she never thanked me.

3 Please pass on my love to my cousin Simon Carter and his family at Peasenhall and to tell Simon I met a friend of his who typed a couple of letters for me while I was at the Savoy a few weeks ago. I can't remember her name, but she was very dishy and she should remember me - the letters were to the Queen and Prince Charles.

4 To Anne, Peter, Juliet and Kevin. Do you remember her wedding and the poor photographer whose camera didn't work? Never mind, as I always say to my couples on Saturdays - what the hell if there aren't any pictures, you're still married aren't you. Send my love to Ireland - I've met a lot of Irishmen here.

Dear kind Rae - have you time to do all this, what with the Citizens Advice Bureau etc.

Many thanks,

Lots of love,

Peter

Peter Hines was one of our oldest family friends. He was four or five years older than me and lived with his divorced and incapacitated mother in a pink-washed eighteenth-century farmhouse in Black Nutleam. Since his parents divorced he had felt it his duty to stay with his mother and would often drop in unannounced at Fulford Mill. He was a great favourite with all of us with his madcap ways and boundless enthusiasm. He made a living as a photographer, specializing in children and weddings and was brilliant at it. At the time of the letter he had been detained in Brixton Prison awaiting a hearing at Bow Street Magistrates Court. An ardent admirer of Mrs Thatcher, he had decided to test the security arrangements at 10 Downing Street. Posing as an official photographer, he had persuaded the policeman on duty to open the door of Number Ten, whereupon he had thrown his camera through the open door, proclaiming, 'There, that could have been a bomb.'

In fact, the only reason I'd intervened all those years ago to prevent the pugnacious Robbie Gordon from thumping him was that I fancied his pretty girlfriend, Liz Baker, myself. I optimistically imagined that casting myself in the role of peacemaker would stand me in good stead next time I heard her high heels clicking down the lane and I rushed round to the front gate to attempt to engage her in conversation, as she walked to her job at Black Nutleam Hospital.

Blushing at my teenage deceit, I opened the next drawer. It too was crammed with letters. These were all from us three children to our parents in the years when we had been away at boarding school. After leaving St Margaret's, the kindergarten run in the stables of the enormous Georgian Hall in Gosfield, by the beautiful, but formidable Mrs Lowe, Ann and Juliet had progressed at the age of 11 to New Hall, a convent boarding school in a stone-built Tudor manorhouse run by Roman Catholic nuns in the village of Boreham outside Chelmsford. It had been given by Henry VIII to Anne Boleyn and was cut off from the outside world by a dead-straight, two-mile drive, intersected by the Colchester to London railway line.

I remembered going to collect them with my parents, at the end of one term when my school had broken up a few days before theirs, and walking across the vast expanse of manicured lawn, studded with ancient cedar trees. We stood in the doorway looking down the long hall, covered with parquet flooring, which gleamed with a highly polished sheen. Juliet had told us that the standard punishment for any wrongdoing was half an hour's floor polishing. It seemed a clever way of maintaining discipline and getting the housework done.

The girls were forbidden to run, not only for reasons of decorum, but also, I suspect, for reasons of personal safety. As we stood there, waiting for Anne and Juliet to appear from the recesses of the school, one over-exuberant young lady, in her red-pleated skirt, came bounding in through the open front door, caught her foot on the corner of a trunk, fell and skidded backwards on her knickers, with a startled expression on her face, the full length of that gleaming surface. She was still accelerating as she disappeared through the open door of the refectory beyond, under the benign smile of the Mother Superior, who was coming to greet us.

Since she had clearly put in her share of floor polishing, I wondered if this was the only recorded occasion of the crime and the punishment taking place simultaneously.

In my case, I left St Margaret's at the age of seven and, three days after my eighth birthday, my parents drove me down to Hastings on the Sussex coast and left me to the tender mercies of Mr E K Barber and his white-haired wife, who ran a prep school for boys called Summer Fields in a large, mock- Gothic country house surrounded by fifty acres of woods and playing fields. I remained there for five years from the ages of eight to 13 and then spent a further four and a half years at Eton.

The long school terms away from home for all three of us meant that the only way of remaining in touch with our parents was by letter. At this time, the telephone was still a luxury to be used only in cases of direst emergency. In my case it was compulsory at Summer Fields for the boys to write to their parents every Sunday morning after church and it was a habit which remained with me throughout my days at Eton. The girls had a similar rule at New Hall.

Anne and Juliet spent approximately six years each at New Hall and I spent a total of nine and a half years at my two boarding schools. I estimated that these 21 and a half combined years of school terms, averaging 12 weeks each, contained 774 Sundays. The drawers contained 512 letters. Each bundle from the respective children was neatly tied with the pink ribbons which used to tie the solicitors' briefs of my father's cases. Wondering for a moment what had happened to the missing 262, I opened a letter from Anne and was interested to learn that in 1953 Lax was Jolly good fun, but Sister Mary Dismus had been highly critical of her essay. Lax was the slang that the girls used to describe the compulsory sessions of lacrosse. Fortified by this useful piece of information, I opened a letter from myself dated October 1957. I discovered that I was captain of football and was bemoaning the fact that, on the wet and windy previous Saturday, we had lost 2–3 to Westerleigh at home. I was convinced that Cooper had scored an equalizing goal in the last minute, but Dats (Mr Standring, our games master and the match referee) had disallowed it for offside. I remembered the incident quite clearly from the distance of 36 years. I had moved forward from my position at centre half and was level with the play, as Simmons made his through pass. There was still no doubt in my mind that Cooper had been played on side by the Westerleigh fullback. Dats with his pebble glasses and extreme myopia, an unfortunate affliction in a games master, was as renowned for his idiosyncratic offside decisions at football as he was for his unconventional LBW decisions at cricket.

Reflecting ruefully on the injustices of history, I read on to discover that I was running out of sweets and would be grateful for reinforcements of Mars Bars and those lollipops that Foster's mother had discovered in the sweet shop in Chelmsford. In helpful self-interest I added the address.

Opening the next drawer, I came across my mother's love letters to my father. This came as something of a shock. Thinking of my mother's neat, middle-aged appearance (she always seemed middle-aged to me), her smart Tricoville suits, her elegantly coiffed and softly waved grey hair, her pearl necklace and her air of quiet sensibility, I found it hard to imagine that she had ever experienced the giddy emotions of youth. Could she truly have written on 11 December 1936:

Darlingest One,

I'm so terribly sorry about that letter, darling. When I'd posted it, I wished I hadn't and had followed your example by tearing it up. I felt miserable coming home after our lovely weekend I suppose and rather disappointed about

nothing in particular. But I'm really contrite, Willie, especially if it upset you, after your nice letter this morning. It
was a nice one, darling. It was lovely to know you want to
have me about when I long to be with you too.

I feel I'm being fussy about the bags Willie, and hope it
won't be a lot of bother for you to take them back. They are
very nice, but not the sort of things you would give me. I've
had such perfect presents from you, I couldn't bear to have
something that was only rather nice - do you understand or
does it sound beastly? The things you've given me I love
almost as much as I love you.

Is the tummy all right again now Willie? Veeraswamy's
will have a black mark on the list for that.

Be patient with me darling because one day you may
make me quite a nice person. I want so very much to be
everything to you and it seems such a hopeless dream
when I'm such a cad.

I can't write any more Willie, or you'll think I'm foolish
as well.

Such heaps of love and kisses from your loving
Willie

I sat and pondered this for a while. It seemed something of an
intrusion to be reading my mother's personal correspondence,
but then was it really? Would she have minded? I doubted it,
and the thoughts and feelings within it, both expressed and
implied, were universal. I thought of the letters I had written,
which after reflection I had wished I hadn't, and presents that I
had selected with great care and affection for Annette, which
had somehow failed to hit the mark.

Making a mental note to avoid restaurants called
Veeraswamy's, I opened the next letter. It was dated 23 January
1937:

Willie darling,
I took a chance this morning and after taking Miss B to
Hastings ran up to see Auntie. She of course was thrilled to

the core about our trying to get on with things. I told her you were worrying about Daddy, so she said why not write to him asking for the consent (!) but otherwise just stating facts, ie, that we propose to get married as soon as can be arranged.

Auntie's most emphatic about our not worrying ourselves about Daddy's views (she says the whole family think it is too silly). Besides which, it does put us in an awkward position, always being together and not engaged.

The briefs seem to be pouring in again. Isn't it extraordinary how things come along in batches? It's rather thrilling when you've got a rush on though.

Our affairs get more and more exciting don't they? ... Willie, darling wouldn't it be gorgeous if we could go away for Easter together? That's being just a little too optimistic I know. Don't let's worry and fuss too much about ways and means - once we're married things will come all right.

So very much love, your own,

Willie

Clearly my parents' romance was blossoming and engagement was contemplated. It seemed strange that my father had been concerned about his prospective father-in-law's approval. They had got on very well together during my knowledge of them both but then, in 1937, my father was relatively newly qualified as a barrister and his practice had not grown into the flourishing business that it later became. Perhaps my grandfather just had a natural concern that his daughter could be looked after.

How different their society had been, when a young couple found it socially awkward to be frequently together and not engaged, compared to my own twenty-year-old daughter living openly with her boyfriend and having no immediate plans for marriage.

I found myself becoming bound up with the excitement of their romance, the undertones of parental disapproval, my father's promising legal career and the intrigue of an illicit

Easter holiday. It was better than Barbara Cartland. I opened the next letter:

> The Pages
> Bexhill
> 26.1.37

My darling Willie,

You were a happy one when you wrote your Sunday letter! I wrote to Aunt Lisbeth today and told her the news, but to keep it in the dark for the time being. I hope it will have the desired effect.

Have you got the ring yet, my sweetie? I shall love having it to wear, for Birmingham too.

There's very little to tell you today, Willie except that I wish you were here with me to cuddle. I was thinking last night how amazing it will be when we're able to go away on our little holidays without any bother at all and do just as we like. Milton Abbas seemed to mean freedom and happiness, do you remember?

The new maid came yesterday, so we've been busy initiating her into all the jobs and I've become quite gentile.

Write to me lots, darling one. Always your own, very loving

> Willie

Aunt Lisbeth was my mother's Russian-born aunt. She was married to my grandmother's second oldest brother Walter and they lived in Tonbridge Wells. My grandmother was the middle daughter in a family of six children, three boys - William, Walter and Albert - and three girls - Elsie, Violet and Ruby. They were the children of a successful hop-factor, farmer and entrepreneur named Dennis Gaskain. He had died in 1936, leaving some £600,000, a considerable fortune in those days. Unfortunately, conditioned no doubt by the social custom of his day, he had left £250,000 each to his two older sons, Albert being mentally defective, and the balance to be divided between his widow and three daughters.

Even in those days of male chauvinism, the inequality of his bequest had created family tensions and bitterness. His will overhung relationships within my mother's family like a dark mantle, even in the time when I was of an age to appreciate social nuances 25 years later. Certainly my grandmother was embittered throughout her life that her two brothers had become wealthy people while she, who was married to a fine man who had suffered debilitating war wounds and the ravages of Spanish influenza while fighting for his adopted country, was left with a bequest of £8,000.

Through serendipity rather than by design, I seem to have acquired the post of guardian of the family's documents and I have read the infamous will. Looking at the neat and impersonal typed pages with their unsentimental, legal logic, it was sad to realize how the final act of what must have been an enterprising and energetic life could reverberate down through the years in such a damaging way.

The 'desired effect' which my mother sought with her aunt, as I learned from the next letter, was that Lisbeth should continue with her plan to give my mother a small allowance. This had been proposed when my mother was a single woman and she was obviously concerned that it should go ahead even if she got married.

So cuddling was in vogue in 1937. My mind raced as I contemplated those 'little holidays'. Where had they gone? How had they got there? What had they said they were doing? Had they registered as Mr and Mrs Smith, had they indulged in unbridled cuddling? My whole world shook. Could it be that in 1937 my parents had been young, irresponsible, excitable and in love? If ever I visited Milton Abbas in the future, I promised myself that I would breathe its air deeply and savour the freedom and happiness to be found there.

I was intrigued by the reference to the indoctrination of the new maid and particularly that my mother had become quite gentile. What on earth did she mean? There was in fact a strong strain of Jewishness in my mother's family, through her father. His anglicized surname was Warrens, but his own father's name had been Wahrens. His was an Austrian-Jewish family, who traced their history back to the ghetto of Frankfurt and subsequently the court of Mecklenburg in the eighteenth century. His grandfather, Edward Wahrens, had been a journalist and financial speculator in Vienna and Trieste who was active in political circles during a time of unrest in the Austro-Hungarian empire. He ultimately became chancellor of Austria and on his death, his house had been acquired by the emperor as one of his palaces.

His son, my great grandfather, had come to England at the end of the last century and set up in business as a stockbroker. My grandfather had worked in his father's firm until 1913, when anti-German sentiment had caused business to evaporate and the firm failed. Whereupon, in an action which I had always found impressive, my grandfather had joined the British Army and fought throughout the First World War, rising to the rank of lieutenant-colonel and receiving the DSO for gallantry. During the bloody battles of Ypres, Arras and the Somme, he had been shot clean through the chest, the bullet emanating from his back, been poisoned by mustard gas and infected with Spanish influenza. Finally, at the end of the war, he was invalided home with no business to return to and a nominal pension. Yet, for somebody who had known the trappings of success as a stockbroker, had seen his business destroyed by the anti-German sentiment in his adopted country, who had minimal prospects of obtaining worthwhile work due to his invalidity and whose wife had been passed over in the will of her wealthy father, I never once heard a word of bitterness or regret pass his lips.

What an intriguing couple my mother's parents had been. The one consumed by bitterness at family injustice, the other refusing to countenance a moment of regret. But there had never been any trace of Jewishness in their neat bungalow at Birling Gap, and latke and gefilte fish never featured on the menu at Fulford Mill, so what did my mother mean when she said she had become quite gentile? Had there in fact been some social shadow over her Jewish antecedents in the years between the wars at the time of my father's courtship? Was it a private joke between my parents? I would never know and there was no one living who could enlighten me.

I pulled open the third drawer of the bureau. It was crammed with photographs. I picked one off the top. It was a small, black and white picture of Bearman in the stable yard. He was standing in front of one of the stables. Rom, my father's bay, was poking his head out, nosing at Bearman's jacket for lumps of sugar and Bearman was holding the horse's lips back, so that it looked as if they were grinning at each other.

Remembering my early riding lessons at St Margaret's and the interest in horses which everyone at Fulford Mill seemed to have, I sat thinking of the endless moments of pleasure that this pursuit had brought me.

In my film production days we had had the contract to produce commercials for Bandits chocolate bars and each January for four years, we had gone to the desert behind Almeria in southern Spain to shoot commercials based around the adventures of a black-hatted bandit in the western towns which Sergio Leone had built for his spaghetti Westerns, *A Fistful of Dollars* and *The Good, the Bad and the Ugly* starring Clint Eastwood.

Our bandit was played by Roberto Arnaz, who, while being a fine actor, was not the world's most accomplished horseman. After several hours in the saddle in bandit's costume in the hot sun, he had become saddlesore and in need of a rest. He was finding the horse difficult to manage and both were becoming irritable. We were on a tight budget and time was pressing. Tom called me into action as stand-in to ride the horse up and down while he organized his camera angles. I mounted the beautiful chestnut gelding, which had been provided by the bull ring in Almeria and was also a veteran of several Westerns. Juan, the handler from the bull ring, silently held the horse's head as I mounted. He hadn't spoken a word all day.

'What's his name?' I asked in my faltering Spanish, as I settled in the Western saddle.

'He has no name, señor. You don't need to talk to him. He knows only your weight. You lean this way he goes so, you lean back he goes slower. You put the reins on his neck he goes this way.'

'I see. Thank you.'

I tested his directions, as I walked the chestnut up and down, while Tom organized his camera positions. It was true. The horse responded instantly to every slight shift in body position. I hit the marks every time, just by imperceptible movements in the saddle. Tom was delighted and impressed. I got off and Roberto remounted for a take. I turned to Juan.

'Why didn't you tell Roberto this?'

'He didn't ask. Would you like to ride him? He's a good horse. You can gallop down the riverbed.'

'Perhaps at the end of the day.'

When filming was completed for the day, the crew drove back by Land Rover to the camera vehicles, which we had left in the Western town, while I volunteered to ride the horse back. Roberto was pleased.

'You're welcome, Carlos,' he said as he climbed into the Land Rover, 'he's trouble.'

Juan smiled a toothy grin as I remounted and trotted up and down the narrow canyon where we had been filming, accustoming myself to the horse's gait.

'He must have a name,' I called to Juan as I cantered past him.

'You want a name, you call him Caballo,' he called back.

'Come on, Horse,' I murmured, leaning forward. The chestnut responded by quickening his canter. I remained leaning forward and his stride lengthened. I held the reins loosely and his ears pricked forward, as the canyon walls began to flash by. The dust of the Land Rover swirled about us as Horse opened his chest and then they were behind us, as he burst into a full gallop. The soft sand of the canyon gave way to small, rounded pebbles, which rattled beneath his feet, as we headed down the dried-up riverbed. It was as if I had wings. The hot breeze whipped through my hair as we approached a long stand of thin, cottonwood trees growing on the riverbank. Sensing danger, I eased my weight back, but Horse had anticipated me. Without a break in his stride, he made a smooth turn to the left, jumped cleanly over the low riverbank and continued his driving gallop along a narrow open stretch between the trees and the canyon wall towards the Western town, a mile away.

It was like riding a Rolls-Royce. The Western saddle, with its low body position and long stirrup leathers, blended my movements comfortably with those of the horse. The reins were unnecessary. Horse never dropped his head, and adjusted his direction to avoid rabbit holes and clumps of larger stones well before I had even seen them. His pace remained at a constant cruising gallop as we reached the fractured shale of the valley floor and the Western town came into close-up. I eased back my weight and we entered the wide main street at a canter.

The Land Rovers were still a cloud of dust half a mile away, as they proceeded gingerly over the uneven ground. Horse's canter slowed and turned into a long-strided walk as we approached the hitching rail. I jumped off, tied his reins to the rail and fetched a bucket of water. Horse wasn't panting after his flat-out gallop the length of Epsom race course. His deep chest pumped rhythmically and he was breathing heavily, but smoothly. He drank deeply and calmly from the bucket. Then he snorted, shook his head and rubbed his velvet nose against my ear as the Land Rovers drew up by the catering wagon.

I put the photograph down and picked up a writing-paper box to which a label had been attached reading, E C Perks & Co Ltd Operative and Dispensing chemists, 1 Sloane Square, London SW1 Tele: Sloane 1896. Inside was a clean, black and white photograph of the interior of a chemist's shop. The wooden, glass-panelled counter and cupboards of similar construction, together with the bulbous dispensing bottles and simple, overhead lighting, seemed to give it a date in the thirties. Below the photograph a pile of A6-sized notepaper with a shaded, italic letterheading seemed of the same vintage.

E C Perks & Co had belonged to my father's uncle and, after his death, my father had managed it for a short period, after he had qualified and before his legal practice had grown to the point where it was a full-time occupation. There was a flat above the shop and he had lived there until the time of his marriage to my mother in 1937.

I had often thought what an interesting time it must have been for a young man, with the excitement of the beginning of his own career, situated in the very heart of the capital, where the gaiety of London life, with its society balls, the men in tails and the women in the post-flapper era of empire necklines, was over-shadowed by the threatening noises from Germany, which were destined to cause chaos and confusion throughout the world and to shape the attitudes of a generation.

My father had never spoken about this period in his life in any detail. No doubt he had other things on his mind, my mother for one, and the photograph gave little information.

Below the box was a photograph of a Siamese cat, lying on the teak patio table in the sun. We had had three, Jemima and her two sons, Tiny and Thompson. Tiny, the runt of Jemima's first litter was my favourite. From the outset he had belied his size and acted with a mixture of boisterousness and insouciance, which first intimidated and then bemused his brothers and sisters.

He had grown into a cat of bewitching independence and sophistication, disappearing over the fields for days at a time and then suddenly reappearing for a week of indolence, petting and home cooking, like a soldier on leave, before vanishing again for another adventure.

He used to sleep in my bed and no amount of cajoling or admonishment by my mother would induce him to leave. He would lie beside me under the covers while I read before turning off my light. When my mother came to say goodnight, she would pull the covers back to reveal his recumbent body,

'Out you!' she would say.

Tiny would look at her querulously, turning his head and slowly blinking his china blue eyes and then, in a gesture of dismissal, go back to sleep.

One summer when I was ten, I came home from school to be met by devastating news:

'Tiny has been run over.'

'Oh no, is he dead?'

'No, but he's broken his back leg.'

'The vet won't be able to mend that will he? Where is he?'

'He's in the junk hole.'

I hurried into the junk hole. My mother had put down a round wicker basket lined with a rug. Tiny sat in the middle of it, his back leg in plaster. He miaowed at me mournfully.

'Good lord. Did the vet put that plaster on?'

'No, Dr Dunn did.'

Dr Dunn was an orthopaedic surgeon at Black Nutleam Hospital. He was a good friend of my parents and his son Douglas often used to come and play with me. It transpired that Tiny had ben found beside the lane one Sunday. Realizing that emergency measures were called for, my father had immediately telephoned Dr Dunn. He in turn had roused his anaesthetist from his Sunday lunch and together they had set and plastered the broken leg in the hospital operating theatre.

From the way Tiny looked, I feared for his life, despite the professional attention to his leg. Who could say what internal damage he had suffered? But he was always a fighter and over the next few days he grew stronger. It was a beautiful summer and I used to spend a large amount of each day sitting on the swing seat on the lawn, reading and revising my homework.

One afternoon, I was astonished to see Tiny coming across the lawn towards me, dragging his plaster cast behind him. Clearly he was bored with the junk hole. I picked him up and put him on the swing seat beside me. For the next five weeks that became his permanent position. He would sit there placidly in the sun while I recited sections of Caesar's *Second Punic War*, declined French verbs and read early English history to him out loud. He became the best educated cat in the county.

After five weeks, Dr Dunn neatly snipped away the plaster. Tiny gingerly tested his withered leg, which looked far too frail to support him, but after a few staggering steps he began to get the movement back. In a couple of weeks he was walking capably, if a little stiffly, and after that it was business as usual. His hind quarters would roll lopsidedly like a drunken sailor, as he patrolled his territory. He lived for another ten years, still retaining his independent spirit and every summer, when I sat in the swing seat there would be occasions when his creamy shape would materialize from the hedge beside the tennis court and he would hop up beside me to learn Economics or English Literature.

Finally he began to grow thin and frail and no longer had the strength to prowl through the long grass across the fields, but would confine himself to the front garden, as if he no longer trusted himself on longer journeys. That summer, I was home from Cambridge, having completed my finals, and was waiting to take up my job in New York. One day, I was sitting on the bench by the patio table, when he came hobbling out of the yard and sat at my feet. He miaowed at me quietly. He no longer had the strength to jump up. I picked him up carefully, feeling his wasted body and put him on the table. He stretched out on the warm surface in the sun, looking at me with those deep blue eyes and blinking slowly.

'Do you want to learn about the American Constitution?' I asked.

He closed his eyes and rested his head on the slatted teak surface of the table and silently passed away, leaving a hole in my heart. Suddenly America did not seem so exciting.

Chapter Three

In August 1991, the Greens terminated their tenancy, having found a suitable property to purchase. David Forrest thought that with the property market showing no signs of recovery, it would be sensible to find a new tenant for the house, but at the same time to offer the Mill and Granary for sale as an individual lot. 'It might be of interest to a "special purchaser".'

Some weeks later I was summoned down to meet some prospective tenants for the house. Mr and Mrs Hillier were a reserved, middle-aged couple with a grown-up family. We sat in the kitchen and Mr Hillier explained, 'We have sold our house and are intending to buy a place in the West Country. It's a life-long ambition of mine.'

In an unworthy moment, I wondered if he knew any nurses at St Bartholomew's Hospital.

In fact they were thoughtful and considerate tenants even though they were used to living in more modern surroundings. They took the house for six months and I continued to make regular visits to continue the sorting and sifting of the contents.

I noticed that the word 'weird' began to creep more and more into Mrs Hillier's vocabulary as she encountered the plumbing, the spring-fed water supply, the coal-fired Aga, the enormous spiders and the other delights of life at Fulford Mill.

Much to my surprise, the marketing campaign for the Mill and Granary elicited a positive response. After a few weeks we had received no fewer than seven offers to buy. David Forrest ran through the list of applicants and their offers. I was surprised at the adventurousness of the human spirit that so many people were willing to take on such a major project in such a dreary economic climate. 'The best offer is from Mr Cook. He's a builder.'

But my eye had been caught by another name. Roger Tabor. Against his name had been written 'Naturalist and Broadcaster'.

'He sounds interesting.'

'Yes, he sounds very keen on the phone, but Mr Cook has made the best offer.'

'Yes, but he'll probably turn the Mill into six flats, leading to traffic problems. Roger Tabor's offer is not much less and he sounds the sort of person who would fit in.'

Negotiations started in earnest and Roger Tabor was willing to match the price offered by Mr Cook. It turned out that he was a biologist, naturalist, broadcaster and writer in his mid-forties with a particular interest in cats, on which subject he had written four books and produced a five-part television series. He described himself as 'The poor man's David Attenborough'. He had come to the end of a twenty-year marriage and wanted to turn the upper three storeys of the Mill into a home for himself and retain and conserve the Mill workings on the lower two floors. Since he had no children and would, in my estimation, end up with something like seven bedrooms in the enormous upper floors and since he was also willing to embark on the conversion of 7,000 square feet of space without water, electricity, gas, telephone or sewerage, it seemed something of an understatement to describe him as a mere 'special purchaser'.

He completed the purchase in February 1992 and I had one less problem to consider.

In the meantime in December I had had a call from the Hilliers to tell me that the cesspit was overflowing. I had it surveyed. It had 'come to the end of its useful life'. During the negotiations with Roger Tabor, I had agreed that we would install a new septic tank to serve the house, the Mill and the Granary and with this in mind, I made arrangements for a Portaloo to be placed in the garden of the house by the back door, until the septic tank was in place. Mrs Hillier was unimpressed.

In January I had another call from her to say that the boiler wasn't working properly and that small bits of fur were emanating from the water pipe, where the spring water fed into the scullery. 'We're having to buy bottled water.' She sounded rather shrill.

I remembered walking up over the two fields by the station and crossing the railway line to inspect the spring which stood on the brow of the hill, 30 years before. It had no cover and was therefore a death trap for small rodents. Some years earlier, when the furry remains of another victim had come through the pipe, my mother had resorted to boiling the water. This seemed rather an inconclusive remedy to me at the time, since the 500-yard-long pipe which carried the water from the spring to the house was made entirely of lead and we were far more likely to succumb to lead poisoning than dead rat.

In February the Hilliers did not renew their tenancy.

David Forrest was concerned. He did not wish to offer the house for sale in the continued depressed state of the market and felt that with its new problems the house would be difficult to let. He sounded unusually morose on the telephone.

'Have you got any ideas, Charles?'

'Well, you found a special purchaser for the Mill. Couldn't you find a "special tenant" for the house?'

A hollow laugh was the only reply.

A week later, I drove down to review the position on site. To my surprise, Roger Tabor had taken up residence in a caravan parked in the garage at the side of the Mill. He invited me cheerfully into his abode. With the low roof it was not possible to stand fully upright and the available circulation area between his bed, sink, stove and working area was approximately 18 inches square. There was not room to swing the proverbial cat. Surprisingly he had two, Tabitha and Leroy, both large tabbies. He seemed completely unfazed by his restricted quarters, as we stood chest to chest, talking into each other's shoulders.

'Aren't you rather cramped?' I asked his green anorak.

'Well, it is a little bit tight, but it's convenient for overseeing the work on the Mill,' he replied to my blue, cable-knit sweater.

'Where are all your belongings? In the Mill?'

'Oh no, they're in storage. There's far too much mess in the Mill.'

There was a sudden ringing sound from within the caravan. I jumped, banging my head on the roof, as a long, white fax began to emerge from under his bed. I left him juggling nine feet of fax paper, with the dexterity of a one-armed paperhanger and drove home, mulling over the unlettability of a house with poisoned water and no sewerage. Only somebody desperate would consider it.

Roger moved in in March. He was either an unpaid caretaker or a non-rent-paying tenant. I drove down to visit him in April after he was installed. He greeted me at the lane door.

'This is a godsend, Charles. It was a bit of a problem in the caravan. I've had my things brought out of storage and it all fits in quite well. I've used two of the garages and put my boat in the stable yard.'

'Boat!'

'Yes, well it's only a dinghy really.'

He showed me around proudly. I had a sinking feeling as I surveyed the voluminous clutter. It was as if my parents were still alive and all my efforts to clear the place were to no avail. I couldn't get into the junk hole, the wash house, the dairy, the larder or the first two garages. Once again the landing to Lucy's bedroom was lined with books. I felt like Sisyphus, rolling his stone eternally up a hill, and wondered what heinous sin I had committed in an earlier life to deserve this penance. 'I'm glad it's helpful for you,' I managed weakly.

In fact he turned out to be a wonderful lodger. He was conscientious and sensible and had a great sense of humour. It was a busy time for me in my business and I did not find the time to visit the house so frequently, but we kept in touch on a regular basis by phone and fax. Since he was going to have to install mains water as well as sewerage to the Mill and since the line of the pipe for the water would have to run across the two fields in front of the house up to the corner by the station, which was the nearest connection point, it would obviously be sensible to take the opportunity to connect the house at the same time and end the problems of the spring water. That way the cost would be halved for both of us. The spring water could be terminated at the tap in the woodshed and still be available for watering the garden in the event that the hosepipe bans, which had been a feature of recent summers, continued.

A few weeks after he was installed in the house, Roger sold the Granary to Bob and Vally Hudson, a middle-aged couple of social workers from Southend, with two grown-up children, who wished to convert it into a house for themselves. They, too, were going to need water and sewerage and clearly it would be even more economic to divide the cost by three.

Roger became project manager. He considered the various alternatives for the pipe runs and the most appropriate position for the septic tank itself and sent me plans and layouts by fax. Eventually we agreed on the best routes for the water pipes and drains through the garden and he began negotiations on our behalf with contractors and with the Anglian Water Board and applied for the necessary consents from the National Rivers Authority.

Negotiations dragged on through the summer months and finally I went down in late August to sign the various documents to implement the work. Roger was in a buoyant mood. We sat on the wooden benches on the patio.

'How's the conversion of the Mill going?' I asked.

'It's going well. We've done a lot of stripping out, making a schedule of condition and where everything goes, so that we are sure it all goes back in the right place. We've also been brushing down the walls to remove the lime wash and take them back to the bare brick. That's been a long job. I didn't want Ken to use a sand blaster because the brickwork is soft in places. Tell me, did you ever do any research into the history of the Mill? I've done quite a bit at the County Records Office, but it would be interesting if you had any more first-hand knowledge.'

I considered the question. It was strange that our family had never really carried out any serious research into the history of the Mill or the house during our period of ownership, since the property was obviously old and we all had varying degrees of interest in old houses. We knew a certain amount about the last century of its life as a working mill through Bearman who had worked in it, through Dick Weller who had lived in a cottage at the top of the lane and through Nancy Blyth, the daughter of the previous owner, who had lived in it as a girl from the time that her father had bought it in 1914. But, apart from snippets of information that had emerged from the deeds, we had never carried out any serious research.

'Not really. I can recount to you various bits of anecdotal history, but nothing of more substance. What have you discovered?'

'Well, the present Mill was built in 1780, by Thomas Nottage, one of the great wool merchants from Bradford Street, who bought it in that year. There is evidence within the present building of an earlier Mill which was built in 1709. However, the site of the Mill is mentioned as forming part of the manor of Crossing in the Domesday book in 1086. So it is likely that there has been a mill on the site for a thousand years or more.' I was amazed that the site was so old.

'Have you done any research into its early history?'

'A certain amount, but as far as the present building is concerned, Thomas Nottage sold it in 1804 to Joseph Savill who worked it both as a corn mill and as a fulling mill until 1813.'

I had never been certain what 'fulling' was and this seemed a good moment to fill in this gap in my education. 'What is fulling?'

'Fulling is when you take the woven cloth, which is still loose with the warp and the weft still visible, and you immerse it in tanks, which contain Fullers earth and night lye.'

'What on earth is night lye?'

'Urine to you. Do you realize that this estate would have had a cart going round Banktree and the surrounding villages, buying urine. Perhaps it's the origin of the expression "taking the piss". Anyway, during soaking, the cloth is beaten until it develops a smooth felt-like surface. This was than combed to raise the nap.'

'And what was this cloth used for?'

'Blankets mostly and greatcoats.'

It seemed strange to think of lying in bed at night, covered with Fullers earth and urine.

'How long did fulling go on here?'

'Well, Nottage and Savill were both wool merchants. You must remember that Banktree was one of the main centres of the woollen industry, up until the early part of the last century. It was really only second to Lancashire in the production of wool.'

'Why was that?'

'It was probably because of the large number of mills on the Blackwater. But Essex is also farming land and in 1813, the Mill was bought by Richard Dixon who was a well-known land owner. I'll go and get my list of owners.'

He returned with a file containing the fruits of his research at the County Records Office.

'After Richard Dixon came John Ridley in 1827, James Catchpole in 1848, William Horsnaill and Henry Catchpole in 1863, Harrison and West in 1886, Harrison & Co in 1895, Cramphorns in 1897, Blyth in 1914 and Llewellyn in 1947. Ridley, Horsnail and the Catchpoles were landowners, Harrison and West and Cramphorns were seed merchants and Francis Blyth you know.'

'It sounds as if there was quite a hive of industry here.'

'A mill was a major investment in the eighteenth and nine-teenth centuries. A miller was a man of substance. We know for instance that Nottage had no fewer than 1,200 outworkers ser-vicing his mills. There were at least 16 workers employed in this mill.'

'The part of the house running along the lane, where the study is, is older than the eighteenth century.'

'Yes, I think there were two, or possibly three, older cottages there. You know you can still see an exposed, inglenook fireplace on the outer wall of the house, which gives on to the yard by the wash house. The only mention I have found of them is that they were taken down in 1707, when an oak baseplate had rotted through, and reassembled on a brick plinth. Judging by the age of the oak beams and the type of joints and construction, they were certainly no later than Elizabethan and possibly quite a bit earlier. I think that part of the house certainly dates back to 1500 and possibly as early as 1300.'

'So would Nottage have lived here?'

'Possibly, or he may have had a manager living here. Since he already had a large house in Bradford Street. But either way the Mill was an important investment and the house would have reflected the substance of the owner. I think that when Nottage bought it, he not only reconstructed the old mill of 1709, but also substantially enlarged the house, building the Georgian section on at the front and redesigning the interior of the cottages to provide domestic offices. It would have been a large establishment with a lot of servants.'

'How many servants?'

'There would have been outdoor and indoor servants. Judging by the size of the Mill and the stable yard and cart lodge, I estimate that there must have been five or six carriages of different sorts. There would have been at least two carts or tumbrils for the Mill, a formal carriage for the owner and his family and probably two broughams or lighter carriages for the individual members of the family. That would mean that there were at least ten horses kept in the stable yard. So a realistic estimate of the outside staff would be two or three grooms and at least two gardeners, judging by the size of the garden.'

'What about indoors?'

We went back into the house and stood in the kitchen. The scullery, kitchen and the room, which we called the larder, which gave off the kitchen, had always seemed a haphazard jumble of rooms to me, with their interconnecting doors and separate doors leading on to the passage, which itself was some distance from the dining-room, through the hall at the front of the house.

'Now this is all quite simple,' Roger said, 'this is the kitchen, which was the cook's domain. She would prepare the food here. The scullery maid would peel vegetables and do the washing up in the scullery. Then this room, which you call the larder, was the butler's pantry. He would keep the wine and the glasses in here and had his own sink to wash up the glasses.'

He lifted a section of the built-in work surface running along the outside wall of the larder to disclose the lead-lined butler's sink.

'These fitted cupboards and the dresser in the kitchen are all quite interesting. Judging by the carpentry and the precise fit at the door ends of the pieces, I would say that they were almost certainly put in at the time the reconstruction of the house took place in 1780.'

'Why are there so many doors?'

'It might seem as if there are a lot by today's standards, but in fact it would work well for the age in which it was constructed. The doors from the scullery to the kitchen and from the kitchen to the butler's pantry were both half-glazed so that the cook could co-ordinate the meal. She could see what the scullery maid and the butler were up to, without having them under her feet. Obviously the kitchen had its own door to the hallway, through the passage and the butler had his own door to the passage so he could carry out his duties without getting in the way.'

We moved into the tiled passage, which I had used principally as a roller-skating course as a child and which had always seemed a cold and dark corridor, dividing the house up in a very inconvenient way and necessitating long walks, whenever anyone wanted to move between the downstairs rooms. 'This passage always seemed a very strange idea to me.'

'Ah yes. It is inconvenient now, but actually it was a very clever piece of architecture for its time, when the house was used in a number of different ways and when servants were plentiful. You have to remember that this was a working mill owner's house. In fact it may help you if you think of it as being part house, part office and part canteen. Down at this end of the passage you have the lane door and beside it the study, which used to be called the office. The mill owner would operate from here. He would have his desk and ledgers and papers. This safe was built into the wall for his cash and valuable papers. Farmers and customers and suppliers and the mill foreman would have their meetings with him here. He would only have had to go out of the lane door and cross the road and he could be in the Mill, without having to go through the front of the house.

'Going down the passage you come to the door of the room you call the junk hole. This would almost certainly have been another office for the clerk.'

'Why do you think that?'

'Because of this door between the junk-hole door and the kitchen door. You can see that it closes across the passage and effectively separates the office and junk hole from the domestic part of the house. The mill owner and his clerk would be cut off from the hustle and bustle of the kitchen and vice versa.

'Now you come to the kitchen door and opposite that the door to the cellar on the other side of the passage.'

'Was that important?' I asked, thinking of the coal, coke and anthracite which had always been stored there.

'Oh yes, let's go down.'

We switched on the light and climbed down the rickety wooden staircase into the large, dusty cellar. Piles of damp coal stood beneath the hatch from the lane, through which the deliveries were made. At the far end, below a broken window frame lay a three-foot pile of sand bags, their cases rotting through and the yellow sand visible beneath. Along the far wall stood wooden, slatted racks on which my father used to stand boxes of wine. The whitewashed walls were covered in coal dust and spiders' webs. In true Fulford style the cellar had a damp, dark and lugubrious air.

Roger was in his element. Picking his way through the scattered lumps of coal, he stood in the middle of the room. 'Now, first of all, architecture. You can see that this cellar runs the full width of the Georgian front of the house. It was built at the same time and is in fact the foundation of the house.'

He moved down to the dark end by the sand bags. 'You see this window frame. It doesn't serve any purpose now, because the foundation for the bay window in the living-room upstairs has cut off any light. But that was done much later.'

'Yes, it was put in by Nancy Blyth's father. She remembers it being done.'

'Quite. This window frame though is Georgian. You can tell by the slender glazing bars and the proportions. There was another one at the far end, which has been used as a coal hatch. In addition to that, there would have been at least one and possibly two windows in the front wall, below the living-room and dining-room windows, so that instead of being dark like it is now, this room would have been quite light and airy.'

'So what was it used for?'

'Well, you can see that it has a brick-lined floor, that there are two chimney recesses, that it has a water pipe on the far wall and a proper drain set into the floor below the pipe. Also there is this long, brick plinth running half the length of the front wall. I would say that it was almost certainly the kitchen for the mill workers and possibly their canteen as well. They could come in from the lane door and come down here without going into the front of the house. Being opposite the kitchen, the cook could bring hot food down here quite easily, or she may have had a separate range in one of the recesses. The scullery maid could peel the vegetables and do the washing up at the sink over the drain. The men would sit round a table at one end and could have a fire in the winter.'

'What do you think the plinth was for?'

'Probably for casks of beer. In the eighteenth century, mill owners had to give their workers a pint of ale at lunchtime, by law. This was because it was such dusty work. If you had 16 workers in the mill you would need to keep quite a few barrels available.'

In our day Bearman was the only person who regularly went down to the cellar, to get coal when he stoked up the Aga each morning. He would bring the coke up in two scuttles and rest them in the passage, as he turned off the light and shut and bolted the door, then he would pick up the scuttles and almost immediately put them down again, unbolt the door and peer into the cellar. He would do this two, or even three times while we three children collapsed into hysterics at the kitchen table as we watched him performing this strange morning ritual.

'What are you all laughing at?' he would say with a puzzled expression, as he carried the scuttles through the kitchen to the Aga and we would pretend that it was at some childish joke, to avoid hurting his feelings. I found it intriguing that 200 years earlier it may have been filled with the clatter of plates, the clink of glasses and the warmth and banter of the mill workers, chiding the cook over the day's offering and teasing the scullery maid over her love life.

We climbed back up the stairs and went into the reception hall with its Georgian proportions and elegant staircase, and stood inside the double-leaf front door.

'Now you can see the complete picture,' Roger continued. 'You said yourself that it would make more sense to come into the house through the front door and that is what Nottage and Savill would have done. A visitor would draw up in his carriage at the front of the house and come in the front door into this hall, from where other doors lead to the living-room and the dining-room. A servant would take his coat and put it on the hangers in the passage, closing the door from the passage behind him. Thus the reception area of the house was divided both from the domestic part and from the office area.'

Although I had often felt that the ergonomics of the house would be greatly improved if we had used the front door, it was amazing to hear the history, structure and purpose of the house explained so clearly by someone who had known it for only a few months.

'So how many indoor servants would there have been?'

'Well, there would have been a cook, scullery maid, butler, upstairs maid, downstairs maid and possibly a footman, who may have doubled as a carriage driver. Say about six.'

'No wonder Lucy used to say the house was too big for her.'

During 1992 the property market remained obstinately sluggish. David Forrest was becoming downright pessimistic. 'Of course it's a buyer's market and purchasers want a lot for their money.'

I considered Fulford Mill, with its antiquated lead plumbing, poisoned spring water, haphazard kitchen, unique electrical system, collapsed cesspit, defunct boiler and corridor bathroom, all the things that a surveyor would look at first. It was difficult to think of it as 'a lot'.

I began to contemplate the prospect of owning the Mill for ever and spending my life commuting from Surrey to Essex on the M25.

The plans for the installation of the new septic tank and the connection of the mains water were going ahead. The trenches, which would be dug along the paths in the garden, and the damage which would be done to the front garden when the large septic tank was installed would make the place look even worse.

Over the years I had developed the habit of making all my major decisions in the bath. I suppose the absence of the telephone and the hot water enabled me to relax and contemplate the issues calmly. I lay in my bath one evening in October, realizing that Annette's roast dinners would have to be curtailed if I wished to remain in eye contact with my willy.

I decided to take the house off the market again. Since it was going to look terrible anyway for a considerable time, until the reinstatement work was completed, I might as well use the time to carry out some basic, additional alterations in order to make the house less daunting a prospect for a purchaser in the hope that the spring would see some recovery in the market.

I knew from long experience what the main problems with the house were and also how its innate, period character could be brought out and its beautiful setting displayed. The next day I wrote to Anne and Juliet in Dublin and Canada in my capacity as executor. I wasn't quite sure what tone to adopt and eventually decided on a light-hearted approach.

Dear Anne and Juliet,

I know that you will be pleased to hear that, in the middle of the worst property slump in living memory, the executor has decided to become a property developer and carry out extensive alterations at Fulford Mill.

It is proposed that the landing window over the lane

door which was blocked up 150 years ago to avoid window tax will be reinstated. The new window will be constructed by master craftsmen to the original Georgian specification. The chancellor has assured me that restoring window tax is a low priority for his next budget. In keeping with the original layout of the house at the time of the addition of the Georgian section, the front garden will be returned to its function of a carriageway by turning it into a gravelled forecourt and parking area. The cost will be considerable. The bathroom will be dismantled and the stained, chipped but irreplaceable, six-foot, cast-iron bath will be carted away. A new bathroom will be formed by knocking down the partitions between the rear landing, WC and sewing room. Taking advantage of the heating and plumbing firm which will be on site to carry out these works, the defunct boiler in the wash house will be replaced, thereby ending the happy memories of the chilly lino in your old bedroom and installing some warmth into the house.

Finally, in order that the grounds too shall not escape the encroachment of the twentieth century, the three-acre garden will be divided in two by erecting a fence from the stable yard door to the tennis court. Many well established docks, nettles, ragwort and ground elder will be destroyed and the land made available as an extension of the paddock, giving access to the stable yard.

No guarantee is offered that these works will be carried out within budget or on schedule, but I know that as executor I can count on the unanimous support of my fellow beneficiaries. Please write to confirm same.

Without Prejudice, subject to contract, but with fond wishes,

Charles

I was working as a consultant on a holiday resort development near Ocho Rios in Jamaica and the next morning I left Gatwick on a British Airways flight for Montego Bay to fulfil my professional obligations while I waited for their replies. I returned a week later and a neat typed envelope from Dublin and a fax from Canada awaited my return.

I stood in my office, in the outbuildings in the farmyard at home, with Pavarotti unravelling my jet lag. The mechanism which cuts off each page of faxes which are received by my machine had broken and several had arrived during my absence. They stretched in a long, white, unbroken ribbon from the machine, across the floor and somehow had managed to slide under the door on the other side of the room which leads down a small flight of wooden stairs into a paddock. On the second step I found Juliet's mud-splattered reply from Canada. Amid a cheerful recounting of her family news was a brief sentence: 'The alterations at Fulford sound great; we won't want to sell it!'

I read Anne's typed, two-page letter from Dublin. It, too, was full of family news. She, too, had obviously considered my proposals carefully. 'I think your ideas for doing up Fulford are great, we won't know the old place.' What great sisters they were. Was this casual approval a family trait or were they latent property developers themselves?

How was I going to orchestrate the work which I had volunteered to undertake? That was the next question.

Having failed to satisfy the examiners at the University of East Anglia, Talfryn was currently unemployed and living in Norwich. He agreed to go down and stay at Fulford Mill to liaise with the various contractors and authorities and took up residence in the first week in December. We stayed in contact by phone.

'What do you want to do first, Dad?'

Anticipating that I would eventually have to go down and spend some time at Fulford Mill myself, I selfishly considered my creature comforts.

'I should think the bathroom is the top priority.'

'Well, Henry Morgan is the man,' Talfryn replied.

'Who's he?'

'He's Roger's plumber.'

Knowing that Roger was carrying out extensive heating and plumbing work in the Mill and that in his usual, diligent way he would have investigated the local contractors thoroughly, I readily agreed that Henry Morgan should quote for the plumbing work in the house. Having converted many houses myself and employed several cowboys masquerading under the title of plumber, how could I resist one who so shamelessly operated under the name of England's most famous pirate?

'He sounds perfect. What about the window?'

'Well, we do have to get planning permission. I've spoken to Brenda Watkin, who is the county planning officer in charge of listed and historic buildings. She's all for it and says there won't be any trouble in getting planning consent, but I've got to take some photographs and submit them with the application. Apparently it will take about a month for the consent to come through.'

'And what about getting the window made?'

'I've spoken to Roger about that too. He's having some staircases made for the Mill and he's looked into the joinery companies in the area. He's using a company in Yeldham who he says are very good. They're called JSR Joinery and they're run by a man called James Townsend. Shall I give him a call?'

I remembered James Townsend well. We had been at St Margaret's together between the ages of five and eight and had remained in touch through local parties in our teenage years. His family had owned the ladies and men's outfitters in Banktree High Street. I was surprised that he had graduated from bespoke suits to bespoke windows but, remembering his careful and sensible approach to life, I could imagine that it suited him.

'Yes, give him a call. I know him well and I think he would do a very good job.'

'OK. What do you want me to do?'

'What do you mean?'

'Well, do you want me to do any work around the place?'

I thought for a moment. Talfryn was young, strong and enthusiastic. He could start making a pile of the redundant metal around the place in preparation for a skip, but would his definition of rubbish be any more certain than mine? The garden was hopelessly overgrown, but could he tell the difference between cotoneaster and ceanothus and would the japonica recover from his exuberant approach to pruning? I'd also learned that he likes to take a selective approach to the job in hand: after a vigorous start in which the job is half-completed, he likes to take a little time off, visiting friends, while the job matures, prior to his sub-contractors completing it.

'Well,' I said, hesitantly, after a moment's pause, 'you could pull down the potting shed.'

'Consider it done,' he said, putting down the phone.

I went down a week later to see how he was getting on. He greeted me gleefully as I parked my car on Roger's hard standing.

'Hi, Dad. We have found a classic example of Millitis. We've kept it because we knew you'd be impressed.'

He led me into the courtyard and proudly showed me an old biscuit tin, which had been cut down to half its original size. A thin rubber hose was inserted in one end and the sides of the tin neatly folded back on each other to form a watertight container.

'We found it in the junk hole,' he said leading me into the house and pointing out a wooden shelf, which had been constructed between two of the exposed beams in the ceiling.

'Look, it goes here. What must have happened is that this lead pipe must have leaked at some stage and rather than repair it, Grandad or Bearman or someone put up this tin to collect the drips and then they would run out through the pipe to this down pipe in the wall here, where the connection doesn't quite meet. Look, the rubber pipe fits in like this.'

'Hm, interesting,' I said non-committally.

'Interesting! It's a classic. I've awarded it the Gold Star of Millitis.'

'I'm sure it's worthy of the honour,' I said.

I had constructed the device myself, 35 years earlier, when I had finally grown weary of the drips of cold water on the back of my neck as I concentrated on my fretwork at the bench underneath the offending pipe. But I knew years ago that Millitis was contagious.

'How are you getting on outside?' I said, changing the subject.

'We wandered out into the garden and walked up the path to the stable yard. The back of the potting shed had been dismantled, but the rest of the wooden construction hung disconsolately by the remaining three sides.

'I thought we were going to "consider this done", last week?' I murmured.

'Yes, yes, but I had to go and see some friends in Bishop's Stortford on Wednesday and they wanted me to stay until Thursday and then I got interested in the drains in the stable yard.'

'Why were you interested in the drains?'

'I couldn't work out where they ran to.'

'They run into this soak-away,' I said, pointing out the two-foot, brick-lined gully.

'What's that for?'

'To let the water soak away, as the name suggests,' I said, surprised by his obtuseness, since he has the sort of brain which normally picks up information without apparent effort, like a dark suit picks up dandruff. Or was I being diverted? Never mind. He considered this arrangement thoughtfully for a moment, then said cheerfully, 'Perhaps we'd better finish pulling down this shed. What was it for Dad?'

Admiring his skills in recruiting me as his assistant by the use of the word 'we', I considered my reply, as we began to dismantle the roof and pile the rot-infested planks on the path. Was it a potting shed? No plants were ever potted there. Was it a tool shed? The garden tools were usually kept in the woodshed. The wheelbarrows were kept in it, along with piles of old sacks, twine, grubbers and defunct mowers.

'It was a bolt-hole,' I ventured finally.

'A bolt-hole. What for?'

'I used to come and hide here before church on Sunday. Then when my father called out for me to join him for church, he wouldn't be able to find me and would give up and go without me.'

Talfryn laughed at my subterfuge.

'I used to find the Reverend Crichton very daunting,' I added lamely.

In fact the reason was that I found Crossing village church a singularly uncomfortable and uninspiring place. The pews were made of a wood which had all the flexibility of slate. The seats were set at an exact right angle to the backrest, so that I spent most of the hour-long service squirming to get into a comfortable position, much to my father's irritation. He, by contrast, sat bolt upright next to his burnished and crowned sidesman's pole. I found it unimaginable that it had ever been used for its original purpose of waking slumbering members of the congregation. It would have taken Rip Van Winkle to nod off on those pews.

The Reverend Crichton had been, what my father called, 'High Church' and used to douse the church liberally with incense before, during and at the end of the service, so that not only did I feel nauseous from the bitter aroma, but frequently had difficultly in making him out, amidst the billowing clouds of smoke.

None of this was conducive to retaining the interest of a young boy and the solemnity, with which the Reverend Crichton pronounced his message from the pulpit, was a further deterrent. It might have been different if there had been a congregation worth speaking of, but the choir of five normally outnumbered the assembled parishioners, the rest of the Crossing inhabitants fearing the damage to their lungs from the incense more than the damage to their souls from missing church.

Father, though, was a dedicated churchgoer. At first he insisted that we three children accompany him to service on Sunday morning but, as I resisted more and more, he was forced to threaten, cajole, bribe, and finally to reason, and discussion became strained and uncomfortable as 11 o'clock approached, until I discovered the potting shed.

I found I had an unexpected ally in my heathen attitude. My mother was neither a Christian, nor an atheist nor an agnostic. She simply had no interest in religion at all. If asked to join us at

Sunday morning service, she would reply, 'I can't, dear. I've got to prepare lunch.'

My father therefore was on a sticky wicket and over the years the potting shed and the roast beef won.

We finished dismantling the shed and Talfryn carted the planks down to the bonfire site behind the tennis court hedge. I took some tree loppers down into the shrubbery and began to trim the overgrown yews and holly which had blocked the path.

I pulled the branches to the edge of the river and made another bonfire site, on a projecting spit of land in the curve of the stream, then I went down the nut walk to see how Talfryn's bonfire was progressing. He clearly was not destined to become an arsonist. Instead of a blazing inferno, he was standing in front of a tiny wisp of smoke, which was curling sorrowfully from the bottom of his pile of dry and rotten planks. 'I can't seem to get it going.'

'So I see. You've got too much on. You're suffocating it.'

We took the charred bonfire to pieces and I recited Bearman's instructions to me, when I had helped him to burn the garden debris in the winters of my childhood, as I started to rebuild it on a different spot.

'First you choose a level piece of ground, so that you can get an even draught. Then you make a tent shape with a few small pieces of wood, so that it draws upwards. Then you light the paper. When your tent is burning nicely, you gradually add larger pieces. When it is burning fiercely you can throw anything you like on.'

Talfryn was delighted with the result and happily piled on the planks and other bits of rotten wood which littered the old chicken run, while I wondered if Bearman's simple instructions would be more useful to him than all the Latin prose and chemistry formulae that he had learned at school. In any event, he rapidly became a master of bonfires, setting fire successfully to my pile on the riverbank and enthusiastically scouring the shrubbery for more combustibles.

As night fell, I said goodbye and set off for Surrey along the back road to Witham which runs along the top of the valley. I looked back for a final glimpse of Fulford Mill at the turning by the Plough. Looking down into the valley, through the soft haze of dusk, it appeared as if a row of warning beacons had been lit along the south coast to warn Drake of the approach of the Spanish Armada. I made a mental note to check the insurance policy.

After Christmas, Talfryn rang me from Fulford Mill.

'Dad, the bathroom's in and the installation of the septic tank and the connection of the mains are both going well. They've got the trenches dug. I'm afraid it all looks a bit of a mess, because it's been raining so much. The reason I'm ringing, though, is that I'm going to have to finish here. I've got a speeding ticket and I'm going to lose my licence. I'll have to go and live at Mum's and look for a job I can cycle to.'

His relationship with the police was in curious contrast to his academic interest in the Law. I considered his remarks, wondering which one of them to reply to, but clearly the time for a more hands-on role had arrived.

'OK. I'll come down and spend some time there myself. Thanks for all your help.'

'It's been a pleasure. If I can't get a job, I'll come down and do some more.'

Chapter Four

Early in January I packed the two-tone, brown leather overnight case, which I had bought at Loews, opposite the Prado in Madrid in 1970, when the unseasonal rain, a fractious client and a disappearing film crew had seemed to call for a moment of self-indulgence, optimistically shovelled some papers into my briefcase and drove round the M25 to Fulford Mill. Roger greeted me with a welcoming smile on the forecourt.

'Where do you want to sleep? I can offer you five alternative bedrooms.'

For reasons of sentimentality I opted for my old bedroom at the back of the house, reasoning that the new bathroom would solve the bathing problems of my childhood. I dumped my case on the bed, went downstairs, put on my wellingtons and anorak and went outside to inspect the state of affairs.

Talfryn had not exaggerated when he said it was 'a bit of a mess'. An eight-foot-wide scar in the earth stretched for 400 yards from the corner by the station, where the mains water to Black Nutleam was positioned, across the two paddocks to the garden fence, where it narrowed to a foot-wide trench with 18-inch, earthen walls, stretching up the path to the potting shed. Here, it did a 90-degree turn to the left and ran down, past the patio, to the front of the house, where it joined the other trenches which criss-crossed the front garden to take the drainage pipes and electric cabling for the septic tank for the house, Mill and Granary.

These trenches had been filled in, but in the curious way that trenches have, earth removed exceeds earth replaced and the ground was marked by lines of raised earth and clay, 12 inches high, as if some over-active, giant mole had run amok. The front garden was no more. On the far side, by the riverbank, stood a large, forbidding revetment with carefully constructed, three-foot walls of earth.

It looked as if the place had been used for an illustrated re-enactment of the Battle of the Somme. I picked my way carefully across the wet, ploughed surface, through mounds of brick rubble and broken lengths of oak paling, which seemed to have been caused by the direct hit of a mortar shell on a machine-gun post, and approached the imposing walls of the revetment.

'*Wie gehts?*' I called hesitantly, as I peered over the top. The green fibreglass covering of the Klargester septic tank stared silently back at me.

I knew that I was going to have to put in a new surface-water pipe to take the rainwater from the lane under the new gateway which I had planned for the forecourt. Knowing how pernickety local councils can be about the specification of drainage installations, I had telephoned the local highways department in Halstead on several occasions from home. The officer responsible, Michael Beaver, was never in and never returned my increasingly exasperated messages. Now that I was in the locality, perhaps my proximity would induce him to give me a reply. I rang the Halstead number. Mr Beaver was on a site visit.

I had considered the question of who I could get to help me with the wide variety of jobs which needed to be done and had mentioned it to Brian, the gardener who came in on Saturday mornings to keep the garden under some sort of control, while the future of the house was decided.

'My brother George is out of a job,' he told me. 'He's been laid off by the foundry and can't find anything else at the moment because of the recession. He'd be pleased to have some work and he's a practical fellow.'

I remembered that, 12 years before, George had replaced the wooden footbridge at the bottom of the shrubbery and my mother had been very pleased with it.

'How much should I pay him?'

'You'd have to discuss that with him, but I'll give him a ring if you like.'

'OK, could you ask him to meet me at the house on Tuesday at nine o'clock?'

Next day, after breakfast I put on my boots and anorak and went out into the sea of mud, armed with a pickaxe, shovel and spade and set about transferring the ridges of clay and earth into the deep ruts left by the JCB. George arrived on the dot of nine o'clock, a slight man in his fifties, with a thick mass of dark hair swept up at the front in a Billy Fury hairstyle. He wore a sleeveless, green anorak and dark brown trousers with a knifelike crease, tucked neatly into his wellingtons.

Fearing for his trousers, I felt that it would be risking providence for him to help me in my mudbath and set him to work digging over the flowerbed in front of the patio, which I had earmarked as the future home of the 16 rose bushes which would have to be moved from the border by the hedge when the forecourt was expanded, while I continued with my shovelling.

The mixture of Essex clay and gravel which the JCB had churned up was unbelievably heavy and the rain had turned it into the consistency of molasses. Every stroke of my shovel became a major effort. Drive the shovel in, press it in hard with my boot, jiggle the handle to loosen the clay, pull up strenuously with my left arm to lift the heavy load, stumble round on the uneven footing and deposit the load in a rut. My boots sank deeper and deeper into the clogging mire until finally, with the shovel full, I found I couldn't move my feet to turn round. I turned the shovel over to release the load while I dealt with this new problem. It wouldn't come off. Realizing that I was going to need the shovel and the spade as crutches to support me while I extricated my boots, I picked up the spade to scrape the mud off the shovel. It stuck fast. The two implements, stuck together with clay, became unwieldy. I held them upright in order to prise them apart, using their handles. In my awkward immobility, they slipped from my grasp, falling on the other side of a two-foot mound, tantalizingly out of my reach.

I considered my position. There was no one around except George. I was reluctant to lose face on the first day of his employment by calling for help. There was nothing for it but to extricate myself by my own efforts. I reasoned that it could be done, if I could take my left foot out of the boot, balancing on my right leg, lean down and pull it out of the mud, rest it in a small patch of gravel to my left, swivel round and repeat the process with the right boot.

Gingerly I drew my left foot out of the boot, balancing on my right leg. So far, so good. I tucked my left leg under me and bent down, grasping the top of the wellington with both hands. I tugged. Nothing happened. I pulled harder, there was a slight movement. I pulled solidly. Was it coming? My right thigh ached from supporting my weight on one leg. I pulled with all my strength, my face screwed up with the exertion. With a reluctant, sucking sound the boot burst out of the clay. The suddenness of its release surprised me. My arms jerked up, the boot slid out of my fingers and flew over my head in an arc, landing on the septic tank with a thud. I toppled backwards. To save myself from falling I planted my left foot on the ground. It sank up to my calf in the mud.

'Urgh!' I would have used a swear word, but in the suddenness of the moment, I couldn't think of any.

I pulled my left leg out of the mire. My sock came off. At least now there was nothing to be lost. Recklessly I withdrew my right foot from its boot and planted it in the mud. Freed from the consideration of balance, extricating the boot was simple.

I stood there with my boot in my hand. My back ached. I felt the need for a cup of tea. I looked for my lost sock. There was no trace of it. I peeled off my sodden, right sock and dropped it near its submerged brother. Barefoot, I collected my left boot from the septic tank and hobbled gingerly up the gravel path to the kitchen door. George was digging rhythmically in the front garden. Silently he surveyed my bare feet and clay-encrusted jeans. His expression spoke volumes.

'Cup of tea, George?' I inquired casually.

'That would be nice.'

Inside the house, I put the kettle on and picked up the telephone. Michael Beaver was on a course.

The original carriageway in front of the house had formed a sideways horseshoe shape, which had permitted carriages to enter at the lower end of the horseshoe, deposit their occupants by the front door and leave by the top end. Each end of the shoe gave on to the lane, from which it was separated by a pair of double-leaf oak gates, some four feet high and three feet wide, forming an opening of six feet in all, at each end.

Between the two gates ran an oak post and rail fence. Between the fence and the lane was an 18-inch ditch, which was designed to take the run off from the lane after rain. The lane rose in a gentle slope from the Mill corner and the run off could be considerable. On several occasions the cellar had been flooded after a particularly heavy storm.

For the many years that the area in the front of the house had been used as a garden, the carriageway had been disused. The gates were still in position, but only the one next to the house was used, as a pedestrian entrance. The hedge, which lined the inside of the fence, had grown across the lower gate opposite the Mill corner.

My intention to use the area as a gravelled forecourt meant that I would have to take down the hedge across the lower gate and reinstate it as an entrance for cars from the lane.

On Wednesday morning I took a pick and fork and, having taken the dilapidated gate off its hinges, dug up the section of hedge and carted it down to the bonfire site. I needed to dig out a section of earth underneath it to continue the line of the ditch, so that the rainwater could flow through it, to spill out into the mill pool beyond. There had previously been a pipe for this purpose, but it had largely collapsed over the years and its remnants would not have been able to withstand the weight of frequent traffic in the future. I needed to replace it with a new pipe of sufficient diameter to take the anticipated flow and to support the weight not only of cars, but also of the de-sludging lorry, which would be coming in future to empty the septic tank.

The ground, which had been compressed by carriages over 150 years and then left undisturbed for another 50 or so, was rock hard. I swung the pick at it and a judder ran up my arms. I persevered and in an hour I had made a three-inch-deep scratch in the surface, the width of the gate. I was sweating in the cold, January air and once again my back ached.

George had made a cup of tea. He wandered out to the front garden with me and surveyed my efforts.

'Looks hard, Charles.'

'Yes, it is.'

'Shall I give you a hand?'

I accepted his offer and we resumed digging as a team effort, I with the pick, George with the fork, clearing out the earth which I had loosened. It was painfully slow, back-breaking work. By lunchtime the trench was nine inches deep and we were both breathless. George's trousers were immaculate.

After lunch I went into Banktree and called in at Thoroughgoods, the builders' merchants. They had some Charcom Safeticurb nine-inch pipes with a three-ton load-bearing capacity in stock and on a special offer. They looked perfect. I ordered enough for our trench and they promised to deliver them that afternoon. Back at the house, I telephoned the highways department to confirm that the pipes met their specifications. It was Michael Beaver's day off.

George and I resumed our team digging. Conversation ceased as we concentrated singlemindedly on completing the trench. Neither of us was willing to be defeated by it. The iron-hard ground seemed like a challenge to our manhood, George was ten years older than I, but he was, if anything, even more determined. My back and shoulder muscles ached unbearably as I swung the pick. Being used to lifting nothing heavier than a telephone and pushing nothing harder than a pen, I had fallen into that state of disrepair that affects so many middle-aged executives.

I began to grunt, like a professional tennis player, with each swing of the pick and I noticed that George was letting out a low groan, as he lifted each heavy shovelful of earth into the wheel-barrow. We laboured doggedly throughout the afternoon and then, suddenly, at four o'clock, it was done. We stood back admiring the finished trench with its neat sides, running the full width of the gateway.

Just then the Thoroughgoods lorry turned the Mill corner, carrying the pipes.

'Where do you want these?' the driver called from his cab.

'Right here,' I replied.

He climbed down and, fixing the straps of his hoist to the pipes, swivelled them down on to the small area of land between the trench and the lane. George watched with a professional eye.

'They look heavy,' he murmured.

I signed for the pipes and the driver departed.

'Well, Charles, I think I'll go and get into a bath,' George grinned.

I looked at the pipes. 'Do you think we ought to put them inside the gate? Someone might steal them.'

George walked to the pile and hefted the top pipe. He couldn't move it. 'If anyone can lift 'em, they can have 'em,' he observed laconically over his shoulder as he turned and walked up the lane to his car. I noticed that his trousers were still in their pristine condition. I looked at my own filthy jeans as I hobbled round to the kitchen door, holding my aching back. Back in the kitchen I pulled off my boots and put the kettle on, nursing the paranoid notion that somehow I had attracted George's share of dirt and crumpledness. Roger's face appeared round the door from the passage.

'Ah, teatime.'

I tried my theory out on him, as I took down a second cup from the cupboard.

'It's either that or else his trousers are of such perfect fifties vintage that the rayon creates a kind of anti-dirt static.'

I picked up the phone. Mr Beaver wouldn't be in until Friday.

Thursday, I had a bad night. There was no position in which my aching body was comfortable. After soaking in a hot bath for three-quarters of an hour, I had gone to bed at 10.30. Sleep evaded me. At midnight, I got up and went downstairs for a glass of Roger's port. At 2.30, I graduated to his whisky. Finally, I fell into a fitful sleep and dreamt that I had been ordered to dig the Channel Tunnel and it had to be finished by the weekend.

I woke with a pale, winter light filtering through the curtains and a dull ache filtering up my spine. I got up and shaved, noticing that my movements were slow and laborious, as if I had been drugged. Hobbling downstairs, I filled the kettle under the tap. It had grown heavier. I looked at my watch. Ten-thirty. Roger came in briskly through the kitchen door from the garden, rubbing his hands.

'Ah, Charles, I'm sorry you weren't up earlier. Mr Beaver has just been on a quick site visit.'

'What! Has he gone?'

'Yes, I didn't want to wake you. I thought you needed your sleep.'

I looked balefully at his scrawny neck, but I didn't have the strength in my arms to throttle him.

On Friday, James Townsend arrived after breakfast to take some measurements for the internal stairs which he was making for Roger. When they had finished checking the details, I joined them on the forecourt as they stood chatting.

'Hello, Charles,' James said, as I approached. He seemed hardly to have changed at all in the 30 years since our last meeting. He was still tall and upright, with a full head of brown hair, a calm, youthful face and a relaxed manner. I contemplated my own, well-worn face, with its furrowed brow, wrinkled eyes and moth-eaten hair, and wondered why the process of life shows so much on some people and not at all on others.

We caught up on each other's news and I was surprised to learn that he too had been through the modern emotional wringer of marriage, children, separation, divorce, loneliness, remarriage. It certainly didn't show. He had married Janet Mackintosh, the daughter of the local chemist, a short, dark, sensible girl and another alumnus of St Margaret's. Remembering her, it was hard to think of a couple who seemed more ideally suited on the outside and obviously they had been for a while.

I wondered vaguely if any couple were suited to spend a life-time together in the fast moving, modern age where expectations are so great and divorce so freely available. I wondered too of the effect on the relationships of the next generation and considered Talfryn's circumstances. Because both Nova and I had remarried and had children and Nova's second husband had two children from his first marriage, Talfryn had one natural sister, one half-sister and one stepsister, three half-brothers and a stepbrother. How could he possibly remember all their birthdays? No wonder I seldom got a card from him on mine.

The following Monday I stayed at home catching up on the post, which had piled up the previous week. Roger rang me in the middle of the morning.

'I just wanted to let you know that Charlie has started dis-mantling the fence. Oh, and the fencing people have started in the garden as well.'

'Thanks, Roger. I'll be down tomorrow.'

Charlie was a carpenter who had been working for Roger in the Mill. He wasn't needed for the present stage of refurbish-ment and rather than let him go, Roger had suggested that he might be useful for me, since he was also a capable bricklayer. He was a big, dark man of 60 with a quiet manner but a twink-ling eye and an interesting collection of hats.

The dwarf wall, which had supported the fence beside the lane, was in urgent need of repointing and making good before it could support the new fence, which I proposed having con-structed from my father's ancient, but still good, oak paling in the garages. The mixture of skills necessary would suit Charlie perfectly and I was pleased that work was continuing in my absence.

I drove down next morning and parked in the lane. The hard standing was full with piles of sand and aggregate, sacks of cement and a jumble of oak beams. Charlie was working at the wall in a gamekeeper's hat.

'Hello, Charlie.'

'Hello, Charlie.'

Clearly form of address was going to be a problem. I decided that I would let him solve it, as I went into the house and deposited my case at the foot of the stairs. I had bought two Double Delight sandwiches at Nutleam Stores on my way through, but Roger was out. I made tea for Charlie and myself and sat alone in the kitchen munching a cheddar and sweet-pickle Delight as I pondered my programme.

Brian and George had together cut down a dead cherry tree the previous Saturday. They had cut up the trunk and stored it for firewood, but the three-foot stump had been too large for the chainsaw. It stood by the cedar tree, an enormous eyesore, so heavy that it couldn't be moved. It would have to be cut up into smaller pieces.

After lunch I went in search of the axe and finally found it in the wash house. I wondered what function it served in Roger's laundry arrangements, as I examined the head. It was suffering from a mild form of Millitis. The shaft did not go right through the head but stopped half way, so that it looked as if the head would fly off at the first vigorous swing. I tested it and it seemed firm enough. By hand, I could neither pull it off, nor jam it further on.

Metaphorically shrugging my shoulders, I took it down to the stump and attacked the lump of solid root-wood, vigorously. My stiffness from the previous week had evaporated with my three-day break at home and I found myself enjoying the physical work.

It was a heavy, silent day, overcast but with the grey clouds high, the air cool but free of moisture. There was no breeze, as I swung steadily with the axe and the slivers of golden wood sprang from the stump.

Bearman had been a superb axeman and I had often helped him, cutting up trees in the willow plantation, which ran in a straggling ribbon of wet, low-lying land below the Mill reach. His stocky body and muscular arms achieved a grace and symmetry, as he swung rhythmically and evenly in his sleeveless, leather jerkin. I tried to emulate his accurate and economical method, so that no stroke was wasted, the bite of the cut a sharp-sided incision and the chips of wood forming a neat pile, instead of scattering over the ground.

By three o'clock the stump lay in four manageable pieces. I went up to the stable yard to fetch the wheelbarrow in order to cart them down to the bonfire site. Charlie ambled across the front lawn towards me, adjusting his mottled green gamekeeper's hat at the back of his head and looking for the wheelbarrow. He stood beside me on the York-stone terrace, looking down the valley past the tennis court.

'Listen to that, Chas. Silence. You don't get much of that nowadays. Beautiful.'

So I was to be Chas.

Roger woke me at 8.30 next morning. 'Phone, Charles. It's Thoroughgoods. Charlie's ordered some sand and cement, but they won't deliver it until you've paid. It's the recession.'

I buttered two bits of toast and ate them on the way into Banktree, a trick I had learned from Edward, now aged eight, who seemed only able to eat breakfast on the way to school. I paid the apologetic manager at Thoroughgoods, hoping that Edward's digestion was better than mine and returned to the house.

I put on my boots and lugged the heavy, blue wooden ladder from the stable yard and propped it up against the house, intending to cut back the wistaria, which grew in profusion around the front of the house and the bay window of the lounge and was curling on to the roof, threatening to dislodge the cast-iron guttering. Roger called from the kitchen.

'Can you go up to Beta Builders? Charlie's ordered some bricks and they want payment in advance too.'

'Don't tell me. It's the recession.'

I took off my boots and drove up Fulford Lane past the triangle to Beta Builders' yard. I was met by Paul Hazel, the proprietor, a short, stocky man with a beaming, unshaven Essex face and a mass of unkempt, grey hair, escaping from a fishing hat of indeterminate colour. He danced around me like an animated garden gnome.

'Ah, you be Chas. Roger said you were good for the money. A thousand reds, isn't it? We'll drop 'em down this afternoon. You just pay Ted, in the hut there.'

I went into the hut and met Ted, a tall, thin man from Hedingham, with a Captain Birdseye beard. I made a mental note not to start a barber's shop in Essex as I made out the cheque. I got back into the car, but Paul was reluctant to let me leave the yard.

'I got everything here. Not just reds. Anything else you want. Architectural and period, fireplaces, cornices, sanitary ware. What I do, see, is buy cottages, convert 'em and keep the bits. No VAT that way see.'

He tapped the side of his nose in the universal gesture of conspiracy and continued to give me the benefit of his advice, as I backed slowly out of the yard, while he walked beside me, gripping the glass of my half-open window.

'Come on back, you're all right. There's nothing coming. Yes, of course the Inland Revenue, now they're different again.'

I inched forward and slowly picked up speed down the lane, until Paul finally released my window and I made my escape with his parting advice on how to complete my tax return ringing in my ears.

Back at the house, I put my boots on again and climbed back up the ladder to continue my untutored attempts at wistaria pruning. It began to snow. In minutes, my fingers had turned white and I was unable to clasp the secateurs. I climbed down the ladder and went back into the kitchen. Frustrated at not being able to get one simple job started, let alone finished, I decided to give up for the day and go for a drive though some of the villages around Banktree, which I had known from my childhood.

I drove along the country lane as far as White Nutleam and turned left, through the ford, up to the main Banktree road. I had to wait at the intersection, while a long stream of cars passed and I remembered how in my youth, it would have been unusual to see more than one car every five minutes on this road.

I decided to keep to the country lanes and drove slowly

through the flat, Essex farmland, through Greenstead with its Saxon church to Great Maplestead on the Suffolk side of Halstead. I found myself driving down the single-track lane skirting Skanes Hall, the beautiful Queen Anne manor house in its parkland setting, where Douglas Hale, a friend from St Margaret's, had lived and where I had spent so many frivolous days. The lane was hardly more than a track now and obviously only used by farm vehicles to judge by the amount of mud on the surface. My automatic BMW swung alarmingly around the tortuous bends and skidded on the sudden rises, until I wondered if I would be able to get out of the lane at all. Suddenly a troupe of cyclists rounded the corner ahead of me and halted my hesitant advance, as they passed on either side of my car, tinkling their bells and waving cheerfully.

I sat looking into the field on my right as they disappeared down the mud track behind me and had a vivid recollection of hurtling at high speed through the hawthorn hedge and turning upside down in Douglas's father's Land Rover at that very spot, 30 years before. We were returning from a hunt ball in Colchester. It had been pelting with rain, but Douglas had been driving with his customary abandon and had been unable to negotiate the corner. After we had clambered, thankfully unhurt, from the recumbent vehicle, lying forlornly on its side, headlights still blazing, and were standing up to our ankles in the cloying mud, futilely attempting to lift half a ton of crumpled metal on to its wheels, Douglas had turned to me and said dolefully, 'My father won't be pleased.'

It seemed something of an understatement to me, who knew his shrewd, stern father well. Then he brightened, as we began the long trudge back to the house, with the wet mud playing havoc with our patent leather shoes and the trousers of my dinner jacket clinging to my calves.

'I know, I'll say it got damaged in the car park.'

I had a momentary vision of the car park of the Colchester Garrison Club packed with Sherman tanks and wondered how he would explain the enormous dent in the roof. Douglas was an eternal optimist.

Emanating thankfully from the lane, I progressed through Gosfield, passing the driveway to St Margaret's, and drove along the side of the large, ornamental lake, built by the soldiers returning from the eighteenth-century wars in Europe, and meandered slowly through the lanes of Blackmore End and Wethersfield to Finchingfield.

This beautiful village, with its Georgian, red-brick houses, mingling with the traditional plaster and thatch cottages of East Anglia, tumbling down the sharp hill from the Norman church to the ford, is known to millions from picture postcards. To me it was known as the home of Jane Miller.

I had met Jane in Black Nutleam Hospital, when I had been taking round the trolley of library books with my mother one holiday when I was home from school. She was in hospital for a minor operation on her foot. I was 15 and so was she. It was love at first sight. I saw her lying in the hospital bed with her long, fair hair fanned out across the white pillow and was hypnotized. I thought that I had never seen anything so irresistible.

At first, my mother was surprised when I developed such an interest in her voluntary work that I insisted on accompanying her to the hospital every Tuesday and Friday when she did her rounds, but with a mother's intuition, she soon found reasons to be busy with other patients when we got to Jane's ward. The library rounds took longer and longer as I sat at length on Jane's bed, discussing the merits of *Anne of Green Gables* and *The History of British Flora and Fauna*, while the rest of the ward, who were mostly middle-aged and down-to-earth country women, made ribald comments until finally, covered with schoolboy blushes like a rash of eczema, I was forced to flee.

After her foot was better, Jane became my first girlfriend and for a year we were inseparable. She was the adopted child of a rather serious couple who lived in a thatch and plaster cottage over-looking the green in Finchingfield. They had adopted late in life and seemed rather old to have a daughter of Jane's age. Whether it was to escape the elderly atmosphere or the confined space of the cottage, Jane loved to visit Fulford Mill, with its rambling out-buildings, its large, disordered garden and its riverside walks.

We would put on our wellingtons after Sunday lunch and walk through the shrubbery, climb through the fence at the bottom of the nut walk and follow the slowly meandering river through the pasture meadows to the mound, retracing the steps of our blackberry-picking walks with Lucy. If it was raining, we would potter for hours in the cavernous Mill building with its massive, lime-washed oak beams, its grinding stones, its steep, narrow staircases and its deep, wood-lined cornbins, while I attempted to explain with my limited knowledge how it had all worked and Jane listened with that apparent interest that comes so naturally to females.

One Sunday, when it was raining, we climbed up into the hayloft on the first floor of the Granary and I was giving a faltering dissertation on the workings of the Victorian chaffcutter, installed among the bales of hay, by the door overlooking the lane, when Jane murmured, 'Never mind that, darling,' and slid her arms around my neck.

Darling! Who was that? Her soft lips found mine and we kissed with the loving enthusiasm of youth. Used, as I was, to the hard, bony bodies and sweaty smells of the rugby scrum, this was a shock and a revelation. Her body was soft and yielding, with lumps and curves in curious places. I was intoxicated by the sweet, lingering scent of her, as she stood so close, neither of us wanting the kiss to end.

I returned to school in confusion and amid the preparations and revision for A levels, wrote long, rambling love letters and waited impatiently downstairs at seven-thirty in the morning for the postman to deliver the blue envelopes in her clear, sloping handwriting. My hormones were in a state of constant agitation.

Sadly, the lengthy separations of school terms brought our romance to an end and I received a gentle, but formal, letter, telling me that she had met someone else, who had a job. How could I compete with employment?

Turning left over the small, red-brick bridge by the duck pond, I drove slowly through Bardfield and Bardfield Saling, appreciating the hamlets clustered around their ancient churches in the long, Essex landscapes, where you could see a wood in its entirety from a mile away, with clearly defined borders, instead of the straggling ribbons of brush or the small triangles of trees between the intersections of roads, which are so common as you approach London.

Driving through these peaceful villages and their interconnecting lanes, I was reminded by the luxuriant hedgerows of the ancientness of Essex. Under King William, the Forest of Essex was designated a Royal Forest. It had to be managed and maintained by the landowners in such a way as to permit the king to hunt it at his pleasure. The noblemen, who owned it were not permitted to turn it into arable, their dogs had to be hambled so that they could not chase the king's deer, no fences could be erected and trees had to be pollarded and not coppiced so that the deer could have free access.

Over the years, the nobleman and peasants nibbled away at this vast tract of forest land, culminating in the destruction of Hainault forest in six days in 1871 by the mechanized Victorians, so that all that is left today of the wild wood is Epping Forest. However, since the paths and tracks through the original forest have largely remained unchanged and become today's country lanes, their hedgerows are often those which were cut from the wild wood and date back a thousand years or more.

The memorabilia of this older history are littered throughout the county. The name of Brentwood is a derivation of Burnt Wood, where the wood was burned to create a clearing for a village. Even in the centre of Romford, where the Essex farmland has given way to metropolitan sprawl, there is a milestone giving the distance to London. Schoolboys sit on it, kicking their heels as they wait for the school bus, unaware that it was put there more than 600 years ago.

Passing through Rayne on the arrow-straight remnants of Stane Street, constructed by the Romans, 800 years before King William, to run from the port of Chichester on the south coast to their capital at Camulodunum, now Colchester, and which coincidentally on its southern section also formed the farm track leading to our house in Surrey, I entered Banktree from the west and parked in Sainsbury's car park to buy supplies, thinking how convenient it would be fo me if Stane Strcct still existed.

Next morning the snow had lifted. After breakfast, observed dispassionately by Tabitha, I pulled on my boots, picked up the aluminium branch loppers and stood outside the bay window, surveying the viburnum in the centre of the lawn between the house and the tennis court.

In my childhood, a 70-foot fir tree had stood in this spot, until, during one gale in the late seventies, it had been blown down. My mother had replaced it with a viburnum shrub with white, sweet-smelling flowers. Since her death in 1986, the shrub had never been properly pruned and it now stood 10 feet tall and 12 feet in diameter, dominating the lawn and obscuring the view from the bay window with its chaotic growth.

Even to my laissez-faire eye, it needed drastic pruning. I approached it with the loppers in hand, wondering where to begin. Getting at it was the first problem. It was even bigger in close-up than it had been in long shot. The growth was so thick that I could not penetrate it to get at the branches.

I walked round it, trying to see if there was a weak spot in its defences anywhere. The only weakness that I could perceive was a small indentation in its perimeter, where a self-seeded hazel had taken root and developed a sturdy growth of its own. I reached in, lopped through the hazel and pulled out the five-foot sapling, leaving the glimmer of an opening. Gingerly I stepped into the opening, caught my boot on a low-lying branch of the viburnum and dived headlong into its tangled interior. The branch loppers slipped from my grasp and shot through the shrub, an Exocet with a toughened, steel head. Fortunately there was no one about.

Winded and scratched, I collected my senses. I was lying folded over on a branch as thick as my wrist. A briar, which was growing at the foot of the viburnum and up through its branches, was wrapped around my neck. The branch above and the trunk of the viburnum prevented me from bringing my arms round to release it.

Its thorny tendril was fixed firmly in my anorak. The only way to extricate myself was in the same direction by which I had entered.

I drew myself back carefully. The briar tore my anorak and scratched my neck and right cheek, but finally I was upright again. I backed out of the recess of the shrub and surveyed the damage. None to the viburnum, quite a lot to me. A row of welts was forming on my right cheek and globules of blood dribbled down my neck. The tear in my anorak revealed a curious grey, foamy lining.

I walked over to the rose bed and picked up the branch loppers while I reviewed my strategy. Clearly I needed expert advice. I went back into the kitchen and noisily put the kettle on. Within seconds, Roger's face appeared in the doorway. He has a Pavlovian response to tea being brewed. Why this should be so is a mystery, since his idea of a cup of tea is to immerse a tea bag in boiling water for a fraction of a second and then fill half the cup with skimmed milk. The resulting brew is a deathly, grey colour and entirely devoid of taste.

'Ah, dangerous work this gardening,' he said, observing my battle-scarred appearance.

'Yes, I could do with some help,' I replied, swallowing my pride. 'You know a bit about plants, don't you?'

We went out into the garden, tea mugs in hand. Roger surveyed the viburnum.

'It is a bit of a triffid, isn't it?'

'What do you suggest?'

'Well, why don't we just give it a haircut?'

He collected some secateurs from the wash house and together we attacked the shrub from the outside. In little more than half an hour it was greatly reduced in size and was an authentic shrub shape.

I went into the house and surveyed it from the bay window. It fitted neatly into the gardenscape and no longer obscured the view past the tennis court.

'Thanks, Rog.'

'You're welcome.'

Encouraged by the success with the viburnum, I looked around for further horticultural challenges and my eye lit on the drainage pipes. Ah ha! In my childhood the paved stone path down to the terrace had been lined with beautiful, weathered larch poles, seven or eight feet high, up which grew rambling roses. Over the years the poles had rotted and collapsed and one or other of my parents had asked Bearman to replace them.

However, for some unaccountable reason, instead of replacing them with similar poles, which would have been readily available, he had constructed poles of the same height out of lengths of unused field drainage pipes, cemented together around iron bars to hold them erect. They were a ghastly, pink clay colour and seeing them sticking up in a regimented line reminded me of a brickworks.

Someone in authority had clearly shared my revulsion, because an attempt had been made to disguise their ugliness by painting them dark green. Nothing, however, could disguise their corrugated, drainage-pipe shape and, over the years, the green paint had peeled away until now they were once again revealed in their full awfulness. For years I had yearned to pull them down, but had refrained from mentioning it, for fear of offending whichever of my parents had sanctioned this eyesore. Now at last I could pull them down without risk of offence.

I rested my hand on the first one and pushed. It moved slightly. I pushed harder and it slowly keeled over at an angle of 45 degrees. I moved round and tried to pull it out of the ground. It wouldn't come. George was watching me from the path. 'Do you want a hand with that?'

We pulled together, taking care not to trample on the rose, which grew around the base. Slowly the pole come out of the ground.

It was astonishingly heavy and slipped from our unprepared hands. I tried to imagine how Bearman could possibly have erected it on his own. He was full of little, engineering tricks for moving great weights and awkward shapes, involving ropes and pulleys and wedges, which he had learned as a lad in the Mill. Together George and I carried it up to the stable yard to await a skip and then we proceeded down the path, pulling up another six. The last one I left. It was almost completely hidden by a former dwarf conifer, which had abandoned its dwarf status and now stood 12 feet tall.

We carried the poles up to the stable yard, stumbling over the uneven, clay mound of the mains water trench, then I stood by the bay window surveying the effect. The improvement was immense. The eye went naturally to the different vistas that the garden offered, down to the rockery with its dwarf, or not-so-dwarf, conifers and up past the hedge by the rose bed, to the taller fruit trees beyond, instead of being arrested and limited by the pipes.

I wondered what to do to support the roses which had been deprived of their climbing poles. They weren't particularly large and they seemed happy enough, but presumably when the growing season got under way, they would need something to curl round and ramble up. I called Roger from the kitchen.

'Rog, we've pulled the poles up.'

'So I see,' he murmured, coming down the path.

'What shall I do to give the roses something to climb up?'

He bent over and examined the roses with a botanist's eye, feeling the leaves between his fingers. Finally he straightened.

'I shouldn't do anything.'

'Why not?'

'They are not of a climbing variety.'

Chapter Five

'All you have to do is to put it on the steam cycle.'

'No, if you don't start the programme at the beginning, it won't be hot enough to cook them.'

Roger and I were bickering about how to bake salmon steaks in the dishwasher.

Liz, Roger's photographer girlfriend, a down-to-earth, Yorkshire girl, clicked her tongue in exasperation. 'You're like the Odd Couple, you two.'

Actually we were more like the characters from another Neil Simon play *The Prisoner of Second Avenue*. We were prisoners of Fulford Mill. Which of us Liz saw as Jack Lemmon and which as Walter Matthau, I couldn't say. Our roles seemed to interchange.

It was an enjoyable relationship, each of us co-ordinating our respective team of workers, he on the Mill, I on the house and grounds, while at the same time, attempting to pursue our respective professions and competing for the telephone.

Answering the telephone was a tricky manoeuvre, particularly at lunchtime. Due to some quirk of British Telecom, Roger's phone would only give four rings before the answerphone cut in. He had tried to change it, but without success. If it rang at lunchtime, when we were in the kitchen, we would both ram back our chairs, like firemen on red alert, and dart for the passage door. Here our paths would diverge. He would scurry down the passage to the handset in the study. I was normally in my socks at lunch, having come in from outside and taken off my wellingtons, and I had learned that the tiled passage was a potentially hazardous surface without shoes, so I took the route through the carpeted hall to the phone in the living-room, as both of us tried to beat the fourth ring and the cutting in of Roger's lengthy message incorporating not only the fact that he wasn't in but also the name, address and telephone number of his agent.

If we failed, the technique was to speak loudly over the message to the caller, telling them to remain silent for five seconds after the message ended, at which point the answerphone would click off and normal conversation could begin. Few callers mastered this technique, normally being too anxious to begin their conversation before more electronic noises unnerved them. The problem with this was that they would then be recorded on the short amount of tape left by Roger's verbose message, until the tape finished, the phone cut off and we would be left talking to each other from different rooms.

'Who was that?'

'I don't know. What does it say on the tape?'

'Hang on. It says "Oh, who's that? What number is that? This is a message . . ." '

Roger had an engaging habit of having a theme for the day. Normally this would begin with an opening statement at breakfast, setting out his thesis and would carry on spasmodically throughout the day as our paths crossed. I enjoyed provoking his accommodating Gemini nature with my more forthright Taurean approach and the conversation would veer off through unexpected byways or obscure abstractions, reminiscent of the junior common room at Cambridge, as he countered my tongue-in-cheek sallies with a barb of his own. He had been a teacher at some stage in his career and had a teacher's natural gift for imparting information in receivable packages. His knowledge on a wide range of subjects was extensive and, like a true scientist, he valued accuracy. If he didn't know something he would say so; but even on subjects where he was a self-confessed amateur, his views were always worth listening to.

Meals were unplanned in true bachelor fashion and occurred on an impromptu basis. When one of us felt the pangs of hunger, we would mention it and collaborate on satisfying it. As befits a biologist, Roger was an extremely healthy eater, favouring yogurt, muesli, skimmed milk, no sugar or salt and so on. He was convinced that with this diet he would live longer.

I couldn't disagree with his physiological argument, having failed O level Biology. I accepted that all things being equal, a healthy eater would live longer than an unhealthy one. My problem was that in my experience, all things never were equal. I could never convince myself that being a healthy eater gave one exemption from the vagaries of life, like getting run over by a bus. I also found it difficult to quantify the increased lifespan or its quality. If it was two hours, would it occur while I was asleep? If it was five years, would I succumb to Alzheimer's and be an embarrassment and an expense to my family, as I lingered on, unable to remember their names?

My mother frequently expressed the wish never to be an old woman. She smoked all her life and it finally killed her at the age of 73. Her death from a pulmonary embolism was quick and relatively painless. Prior to her departure she had never known a day's serious illness in her life. All in all, it seemed a reasonable trade-off.

My father, who had never smoked, had a degree in hypochondria and was the delight of Harley Street, had lived to 82, but the last five years had been ones of loneliness, increasing immobility, failing eyesight and advancing senile dementia.

If it was my turn to organize supper, this would normally be of the takeaway variety. I soon discovered that Banktree had an intriguing mix of ethnic cuisines. The fish and chip shop in Sandpit Lane was run by a Chinaman and the chinese takeaway in the precinct of the Old Silk Mill was run by a couple from India. This confusing arrangement meant that suggesting we had a Chinese takeaway was something of a problem. If Roger was buying and I fancied Chinese, I, who cannot stand Indian food, solved it by ordering an Indian, until one evening he returned, proudly bearing a chicken Vindaloo from the Indian takeaway in Coggeshall, which lifted the roof off my mouth. Luigi's, the Italian takeaway in the market square, was run by Roberto from Manchester. The first time I went there, I fell into conversation with him as he prepared my order.

'Which part of Italy are you from?'

'From Napoli,' he said in a true Marcello Mastroianni accent.

'Ah,' I said, remembering the beautiful coast road from Naples down to Paestum from a hitchhiking holiday I'd taken in my teenage years. 'Do you know Amalfi?'

'No, I do not know. I have no visited Amalfi. To tell ze truth, I have no visited Napoli.'

'Oh, did you emigrate to England and have never been back?'

'No, my parents, they emigrate. I was born in Manchester.'

His accent was becoming distinctly Mancunian.

'I have never been to Italy,' he added. His accent only needed a 'Bah Gum' to be truly vernacular.

'I see.' My conversation faltered as he passed me the packages of spaghetti alla Carbonara and vitello Milanese.

I drove back to the house and unwrapped the packages on the kitchen table.

'Right Rog, there's spaghetti Old Trafford for you and vitello Oldham for me.'

'Eh?'

Friday was a brick-laying day. The sand and cement and the thousand reds had all been delivered. The Charcom Safeticurb pipes stood unmolested by the gate. I was anxious to complete the dwarf wall, the entrance way for the new gate to the forecourt and a retaining wall to surround the septic tank before I arranged for a contractor to come in and lay out the gravelled area. Charlie had organized the delivery of a small, electric cement-mixer from the hire shop in Banktree. He arrived at 8.30 in a brown trilby.

'Right, Chas, if you can pass the bricks along to me, George can mix up the cement.'

We fell naturally into the hierachy of the building site where the brick layer is king. When they had started work for me both George and Charlie had treated me with a certain amount of respect. I was the person who gave them their instructions and paid their wages. However, as the days had passed and I had demonstrated my eagerness to participate in all aspects of the conversion work and, more importantly, was the only source of drinkable tea, I was accepted as part of the Fulford gang, which included Ken and Simon in the Mill and David, who had started work converting the Granary for Bob and Vally. There was a community spirit in the hamlet and I was pleased to be part of the camaraderie.

Charlie, who had started off regarding me as a city slicker, was surprised at my adeptness as a hod carrier, as I kept him supplied with bricks and mortar while he progressed steadily along the wall, bending over in the culvert beside the lane.

'You've done this before, Chas.'

'Yes, once or twice,' I replied, thinking back to the holiday job which I had had as a hod carrier in the break between school and university, first demolishing and then rebuilding Felsted College Chapel and the many times in my own property company, when I had peeled off my suit and pulled on overalls to get involved with the physical work. I had always found it a refreshing change.

It wasn't just the opportunity to use my muscles instead of my brain. The culture of the workplace is different from the culture of the office and the conversation reflects this. The office is a place where achievement is measured by the shuffling of paper, mental processes are disturbed by the need to meet or, if necessary, circumvent bureaucratic requirements and all activity is measured by the yardstick of money, how to raise it, invest it, spend it. At the workplace, achievement is measured by the completion of a specific task, mental processes are directed towards this goal and activity is measured by minimizing the time necessary to complete it, in order to get to the pub. I had noticed how when my property company had been taken over by a large public company and I had become for a while a member of a sleek, big company hierarchy, that executives would hustle around the building, carrying bundles of files on some apparently urgent mission. Occasionally they would come into my office and say:

'Charles, can I just put this on your desk?' emphasizing 'your'; indicating, I think, that the file contained a matter for my attention. There was only one answer to this. I had a big desk. It was always littered with bits of paper of my own and one more file wouldn't make any difference. Besides, their files were always so much neater than mine.

'Yes,' I would say, non-committally at first, engrossed as I was with my own programme, but then with increasing enthusiasm, as I discovered that they never evinced any disappointment, or even surprise, that I hadn't opened their files when they came to collect them a few days later. Perhaps they just wanted somewhere to park them during their ceaseless perambulation of the building.

One thing that did intrigue me was the anonymity of these peripatetic floor walkers. I didn't know who they were or where they had come from. Who had sent them on their expeditions? Did they have homes and loved ones and problems? Would anyone notice their replacement or their departure? Did anybody know them? Indeed, did anybody know anyone outside their own department?

I decided to carry out some field research of my own. I had received a copy of the *Estates Gazette* in a brown, A4-sized envelope. Crossing out my name and address, I wrote Sharon on it in large, mauve Pentel. I put a five-pound note and some loose change in the bottom and then walked up and down the five-storey building. I went into each department and said to the nearest unfamiliar face: 'Oh, Sharon in accounts is leaving. We were just having a collection for a leaving present.'

There was nobody in the company called Sharon and the accounts department consisted of two male accountants and a computer. None the less, by the time I reached the ground floor, I had collected £37.60.

I picked up the phone on the receptionist's desk and dialled my internal number. Lilian, my slim, alert, 60-year-old secretary answered.

'Lilian, I'd like to take you to lunch,' I said.

'Oh, that would be nice.'

We enjoyed antipasti and seafood salad, washed down with a bottle of Frascati at the trattoria on the ground floor of the Grosvenor House Hotel. Over coffee, Lilian said hesitantly, 'What exactly are we celebrating Charles?'

'I've just come into some money, Lilian.'

I tried to imagine Charlie's dusty response to being told that 'Sharon in accounts' was leaving, as we worked steadily throughout the day. He'd probably ask for her telephone number. We didn't speak much, but there was a sense of purpose surrounding our activity. There is a direct correlation between neatness and achievement on a building site and both Charlie and George were neat workmen. If a section of pointing stood proud of his line, as he made constant adjustments, Charlie would go back and redo it. As George broke open each sack of cement, he would stuff the paper container inside the previous one so that there was no litter.

At four o'clock, Charlie laid down his trowel. 'Well, that's it for me today, Chas. I've got to go and see my young lady.'

It was time for me to be getting back to Surrey too. I packed my case, wondering how young his young lady was and drove up to the Lada Lifestyle garage on the Nutleam Road into Banktree to fill up with petrol for the return journey. The garage had previously been owned by Denis Parsons and operated under the name of Morris & Parsons. As I filled up the car I wondered what a Lada Lifestyle was. It didn't sound very inspirational.

Entering the shop to pay, I was surprised to see the till manned by Lawrence, Denis's brother. He greeted me without a flicker of surprise

'Hello, Charles. We haven't seen you for a while.'

I did a quick, mental calculation of when I had last seen him and estimated that it must have been around 1977, when I'd spent a few weeks at Fulford Mill after my divorce from Nova.

'About 15 years,' I replied.

'Doing some work at the house are you? I've seen the lights on in the Mill and you've pulled the old fence down then?'

He continued the conversation as if nothing had interrupted an earlier conversation we had been having in 1977. As he gave me my change, he grinned and said, 'Ivan Roy don't open the batting for Crossing any more, you'll be pleased to know.'

In my summer holidays, I had played cricket for the Crossing village team. I had opened the batting with Ivan Roy, a stocky man in his thirties, with a shock of thick, black hair and the physique of a blacksmith. He could strike the ball ferociously, but he was an optimistic judge of a run. On several occasions I had been run out on account of his injudicious calling. Lawrence, who batted at number six, had witnessed my frustration as I threw my bat down in the wooden hut, which passed for a pavilion, underneath the oak tree at the side of the uneven, grazing meadow, which each summer doubled as the cricket pitch.

I was sorry to hear that Ivan had finally hung up his bat and retired from the game he loved so much, but then Lawrence was talking of a time more than 30 years ago and Ivan must have been approaching 70 by now.

'No,' Lawrence added, as I turned to leave, 'he goes in number three now.'

I drove back to Surrey, imagining an ageing, rotund Ivan going in first wicket down and hoped that he had been blessed with a nimble-footed number four.

The following Monday and Tuesday, Charlie, George and I continued our work in the front garden. Charlie finished repairing and repointing the dwarf wall and built a short return, on which to hang the new gate. George collected the broken and rotten pieces of the old oak fence and carted them down to the chicken run for another bonfire. Together, George and I lifted the Charcom Safeticurbs pipes into position in the trench which we had dug earlier. They were astonishingly heavy for their size and we found that the only way to manoeuvre them was to slide a six-foot fencing stake, which I had found in the stable yard, through the hole and to carry them, one at each end, like a sedan chair. We fiddled them into position while Charlie gave us instructions, armed with his spirit level and twine. Finally he was satisfied that the falls and levels were right and started to cement them into position.

I stood in the lane surveying the effect of our progress so far. The front garden still looked terrible. In fact, now that the gate and fence were down and the entire site was fully disclosed to view, it looked, if anything, rather worse. The pile of earth and clay around the septic tank was a soggy, misshapen mess. The soil from the rose garden had been churned up with the gravel from the paths by the JCB, which had dug the trenches leading to the septic tank, and now lay in corrugated ridges the length of the house, despite my earlier attempt to level them out. The thick, overgrown hedge hung threateningly over the remaining roses at the edge of the flower garden. Charlie observed the disconsolate expression on my face.

'It'll look fine, Chas.'

He climbed out of the culvert, wiping the back of his arm across his forehead and stood beside me in the lee of the Mill, adjusting his pork pie hat on his springy curls.

'Looks a mess now, doesn't it,' he grinned.

'Mmm.'

'It won't do, though. You just can't see it. Don't look at the surface. That'll all go when the gravel is laid. Don't worry about the levels either. We can't do anything about that. There's several tons of earth to be moved there. It needs a JCB. The contractor'll do that. What you've got to look at is the shape. Look, I'll show you.'

He walked through the churned-up earth to the far side of the front garden, where the lawn started its sweep down to the tail water and the path leading to the shrubbery, picking up several pieces of brick and concrete which had been ploughed up when the JCB had dug up the paths leading to the ornamental birdbath, and laid them in a rough line on the far side of the site, curving round in a gentle arc from the septic

The mill workers at the turn of the century.

Mr Weller, the last miller, and colleagues from the Mill.

The same view, fifty years apart.

Further changes over the years.

Looking up from the river to the Mill, granary and Mill house.

The carriage gate.

An early cause of Charles' myopia.

The Lone Ranger and the faithful Tonto.

Sister Juliet, who later emigrated to Canada to perfect her kayaking skills.

The grinding stones.

The old tumbrel for transporting sacks from the Mill.

The Mill in spring.

A prisoner of Fulford Mill.

'My Mill.'

Views of the gardens and grounds.

tank to the corner of the house.

'See. That's how it'll go,' he called across the lane. I could see it at once and was grateful for his understanding. George came to stand beside me at my vantage point. He was a keen gardener, spending most of his spare time in his large greenhouses at home and visiting flower festivals and country shows at weekends.

'The landscaping will make all the difference, but grading, the forecourt is going to be a tricky job.'

Charlie rejoined us from the garden and George turned to him.

'Who do you recommend for the grading, Charlie?'

'Dunno. It's going to be difficult with those levels. You've got to drain it away from the house and away from the lane with the fall of the land, but you can't go too deep because of the two manhole covers. I've got a mate in Chelmsford. I'll ask him.'

George picked up a spade from the gateway. 'I think I'll just get on with moving those rose bushes.'

Wednesday, Roy Lake, the fencing contractor, arrived at lunchtime with the single-leaf, six-foot entrance gate for the forecourt. A fair-haired prop forward in his late twenties, he greeted me cheerfully as I came round the house to help him unload the gate from the back of his pickup truck.

'Hi there, Charlie. Is that fence all right?'

I hadn't seen him since he had erected the post-and-rail fence from the stable yard down to the tennis court three months earlier. He had been concerned about the line of the curve which was necessary to intersect the garden between the fruit trees and a stand of three, large eucalyptus trees and had telephoned me at home to ask for my instructions. Eventually I had decided to leave the eucalyptus trees in the new meadow. I wasn't sure if horses or cattle would nibble their bark, nor if they would be poisoned if they did so, but I reasoned that it would be simple for a future owner to construct an individual fence around them. We walked up to the stable-yard door and stood looking at the line of the fence.

'I think it looks fine, Roy.'

'Just so long as you're happy. The garden looks much better with the fence, doesn't it? This door leads straight into the field now. Makes more sense.'

I was pleased that he approved of the practicality of my design and wondered why it was important to me. Roy wasn't a landscape gardener and he had no first-hand knowledge of the history of the house or of how it would have worked, but he was an ebullient and sensible chap with a cheerful and positive outlook. I suppose it was that the few simple improvements and alterations that I was making to the house and grounds were ideas that I had nurtured for 35 years. They seemed obvious to me, but perhaps they would not to others and I was encouraged by his seal of approval.

After lunch, George was levelling the ground in the forecourt where the trench for the electric cabling for the septic tank had passed under the dining-room window and would be difficult for a JCB to reach. Charlie was up in the stable yard, sawing the rotten ends off the oak paling, where they had rested on the damp garage floor for so many years, before they could be used to form a new fence to go on top of the dwarf wall. Roy's assistant, Dave, had to go and finish off another job, so during the afternoon, I helped him dig the holes for the six-by-six gateposts and set them in position in aggregate and concrete. He worked quickly and efficiently, chattering on about life in general and the recession in particular.

'It's a bloody shame. I've had to lay blokes off, good blokes, but there isn't the work. No one's got any money. It's these interest rates.'

'We have to have high interest rates to remain in the European exchange rate mechanism,' I said tentatively, thinking of how many of my own friends had lost their businesses, their houses and, in some cases, their health and families as well, for the same reason and privately knowing that we would eventually be forced to leave the ERM through pressure of international speculation.

'Why bother with that? Why penalize our blokes? Do you think the French would, or the Germans? Christ we've been at war with them since God knows when. No, they'd find some other way.'

'Well, it won't last for ever.'

'No, you're right. That's why you're doing up this place. You'll never sell it until people have got some money, so why not do it up in the meantime. I'd do the same. You're right, we've just got to get on with it, but it makes me mad when I see the misery it causes.'

The gateposts would have to set into the concrete overnight, so we carried the gate round to the courtyard and I went into the house to have a bath and to change. I had been invited to have dinner with Chris and Jill Johnson and Peter Hines. Chris was Peter's half-brother and Jill was another old girl of St Margaret's. Her father had been a doctor in Banktree. I was a useless god-father to their daughter Virginia.

Chris had spent his professional life working for Monsanto in Belgium. Having recently retired, they had returned to the area of their roots and bought a converted barn in the village of Marks Tey between Banktree and Colchester.

I drove down the winding, narrow lane off the A12 and found the barn at the end, before the lane petered out into fields. Chris greeted me effusively at the door.

'Good lord, Charles. I wouldn't have recognized you. Come on in. Jill, look who we've got here.'

Jill emerged from the kitchen, untying her apron and smoothing her shoulder-length, dark hair.

'Hello, Charles. How nice to see you. Peter's here some-where.'

They had changed remarkably little in the 15 or so years since our last meeting and seemed far too young to have retired. Jill's oval face was completely unlined and although Chris's hair was tinged with grey, it was as full and wavy as ever. They both seemed fit, energetic and enthusiastic.

I was surprised at how sympathetically the 200-year-old barn had been converted and said as much.

'It's a bit windy,' Jill replied.

I wasn't surprised. The dining area was positioned in what

had been one of the opposing floor to ceiling sections facing the prevailing wind and I was reminded how barns such as this had been constructed as winnowing machines as much as store-houses. It was an essential prerequisite that they should be windy, in order to separate the chaff from the grain as the corn was flailed in the centre of the barn.

We ate supper in the kitchen and I took it as a compliment that after 30 years we slipped so naturally into this habit of our child-hood. Then, dining-rooms were the private domain of parents, with the associated formality. Normally the kitchen was the nat-ural feeding habitat of the younger generation. Yet here we were, now parents ourselves, still in the kitchen, enjoying its ambience but discussing our own offspring. Besides, it wasn't windy in the kitchen.

'What's Talfryn up to?' Jill asked.

I gave them a brief resumé of Talfryn's chequered academic career adding, 'He never seems able to settle to anything, and he has such a short attention span. I despair of him.'

Chris laughed resoundingly. 'Look who's talking! Your father despaired totally of you.'

'Did he?' I said, surprised that my haphazard early career should have been seen as anything other than part of a carefully conceived master plan.

'Did he indeed? When he visited my father at our old house, it would be a wailing and gnashing of teeth.'

'Oh.' I felt deflated.

'Still it worked out all right for you, didn't it?'

'I suppose so.'

'My son Richard is the same. He can't settle down to anything and has these airy-fairy ideas, but you shouldn't worry about it. Look, Richard and Talfryn are the last people you should worry about. I've stopped thinking about it. I know that one day Richard will turn up here in a Rolls-Royce that is so wide it won't get through our gateposts. Then I'll be infuriated. The least deserving always reap the greatest rewards.'

'More likely to be a Mercedes.'

Thus relieved of my paternal responsibilities, the conversation turned to lighter subjects. Over coffee, Jill brought out some photographs from St Margaret's days and tested my failing memory cells. When I had finally managed to identify the solemn faces in the school play, she filled in many of the details of their later lives. Finally, she came to some black and white photographs of her twenty-first birthday party.

'And who's this?' she asked, passing me a picture of a dinner-jacketed young man with a lot of dark hair, gesticulating at the photographer with a cigarette in his outstretched hand.

'Clive Ripper,' I said confidently.

'No, silly! It's you.'

'Good grief.' I looked at the photograph again. It struck no chord in my memory. The confident expression, the unlined face, the adoring look on the face of the young blonde formed no part of my consciousness.

'Good grief,' I repeated, appalled, as I ran my fingers over my bald patch in an instinctive gesture of vanity, knowing what it felt like to be the picture of Dorian Grey.

Peter was unusually quiet during supper. His mother had died two years earlier and he had eventually sold the family house and moved to a modern house on the outskirts of Colchester, not far from Chris and Jill. He seemed more subdued than usual and he didn't seem to be taking photographs or pursuing any particular profession, nor did he join in the conversation in his former exuberant and uninhibited manner.

'What's up, Peter?'

'Oh nothing, Charlie. I'm fine. I'm just tired. Christ, I'm over 50 now, I'm allowed to be tired.'

'What are you up to?'

'Nothing much. Trying to sell those bloody Monets.'

His father John, who had lived in the West Country with his second wife, had died two years before Peter's mother. Among his effects had been found eight or ten 'fragments' of paintings by Monet. 'Fragments' was the term which had been ascribed to them by art experts, but to my eye, who had seen them, it seemed to belittle them, since they were quite large. The smallest was some 18 inches by two feet and the largest was three feet by four. It appeared that they were sections of larger paintings that Monet had discarded and not incorporated in the finished work. To my eye they were undoubtedly Monet's and this had been confirmed by the leading Monet expert.

Peter's father, who had had an abiding interest in art, had acquired them after the war. He had visited Monet's house at Giverny outside Paris before it became the art tourist's shrine, which it has now become. There he had fallen into conversation with the gardener, who had been given them by Monet himself. John Hines had brought them back to England in an era before art licensing had become widespread.

There was a study of the Japanese bridge, another of Monet's wife and a section that had obviously been intended as part of *The Water Lilies*. I imagined that they must cumulatively be worth hundreds of thousands of pounds, if not millions, in view of the current price paid for the works of the Impressionists and would provide Peter with a security which would be helpful in the future and Chris with a degree of affluence in his retirement. But it seemed not. The arcane and political world of the art historian had intervened and although authentication was agreed, accreditation of the paintings as pictures, and therefore inclusion in the definitive Monet reference book, was not. Their value therefore was extremely doubtful.

'Those bloody pictures,' Chris intervened with exasperation. 'Quite frankly, Charles, I've washed my hands of them. We'll be lucky if we see a penny for them.'

I had always been interested in art myself and thought that Monet had been a giant among painters. I had visited Giverny three years before with my daughter Celina, and wandering around the long, village house with its pastel, yellow kitchen with the blue-tiled range and the formal garden leading over the lane to the Japanese bridge, I had been struck by how one eye and hand could transform something mundane into something universal and how Monet's individual perception had led to Impressionism. He seemed to me to occupy the same position in French painting that Turner occupied in English and a Monet would go well with the eighteenth-century watercolours that

Annette and I had collected over the years.

'I'll give you fifty quid for the lot,' I said.

'No chance,' Peter snorted from the sofa.

'Would that be cash, Charles?' Chris asked as he refilled my coffee cup.

Replete with the meal, the wine, the memories and the friend-ship, I made my farewells. Chris walked with me to the car.

'Peter seems a bit subdued,' I said.

'He's all right. He's just tired. He's just ridden his 750cc Yamaha down to Dorset and back to pick up his new, all-in-one motor-cycle leathers.'

'Good heavens. What colour are they?'

'Canary yellow.'

Peter was fine.

Monday 1 February.

I drove down in the afternoon, thinking that that way I would at least miss one lunch of Double Delights. As I took my case up to the bedroom I had to step round various pieces of bathroom equipment, the laundry basket, soap dish, toilet brush, a pile of flannels, soap, tooth mugs, shaving foam containers and towels, which cluttered the landing leading to my bedroom door. From inside the bathroom came a soft rustling noise and occasional words of advice, 'up there', 'round this bit'.

I had scoured the *Banktree Times* and the *Essex Chronicle* to find a decorator who could paper and paint the new bathroom and could decorate the corridor which had housed the old bathroom. Due to the recession, there had been no shortage of small ads offering decorating services. I had called several of the telephone numbers, but found that the ads had been inserted by people who had been laid off from other occupations: a welder, a shop assistant, a garage mechanic.

Because the new bathroom was in the oldest part of the house, its shape was irregular and the plaster surface uneven. Preparation was going to be critical, if the imperfections were not to show through when the paper was applied and I wasn't cer-tain that a welder would fully appreciate the finer points of decor.

Finally I found Len, a professional decorator, who sounded sensible and enthusiastic on the phone. He'd come round to price the job up, a fit looking man of about 50 with a mass of long white hair, a pallid complexion and Ken Dodd teeth.

'Yes, I can fit it in,' he said. We had agreed terms and now I remembered that this was the day he had said he would start.

I dropped my case on the bed and pushed open the door to the bathroom. A fine pall of plaster dust hung in the air, like a paperweight that you turn upside down to see Buckingham Palace in a snowstorm. Every surface was covered with a fine layer of talcum powder. Of Len there was no sign. The rustling noise continued and a voice said, 'Around this beam. Up into that corner.'

'Len?' I called.

'I'm up here.' The deep voice replied echoing round the ceiling. I made out the shape of a pair of stepladders, projecting up into the space where the ceiling of the old landing had been higher than the sewing room. A disembodied, pink T-shirt floated down the ladder towards me. I took an involuntary step back at this ghostly apparition. The T-shirt wafted towards me. Then, to my amazement, it spoke. 'It's me, Len.'

'Slowly his outline came into focus. He was wearing white decorator's trousers and white trainers. The plaster dust had covered his arms and hands and, together with his white hair and pallid complexion, had rendered him completely invisible in the white-walled room, like a snowman in a snowstorm. Only the pink T-shirt testified to his mortal presence.

'I thought I heard voices,' I said weakly, as I recovered my composure.

'Yes, I was giving myself instructions.'

Tuesday 2 February.

The morning dawned cold. Len arrived at eight o'clock and beat me to the bathroom. I decided to follow the Essex fashion and stop shaving. There had been a sharp overnight frost and a pale grey haze of mist hung in the valley. As I went downstairs to organize breakfast, Graham was already on the roof above

Roger's bedroom, whistling an improvised version of 'Danny Boy', as he cleared the gutters of many years of pine needles. Another victim of the recession, he had been laid off by Henry Morgan. A roofer by trade, he had willingly accepted my offer of a few days' work replacing the slipped and broken tiles on the main roofs of the house, repairing the hole in one of the chimney stacks and clearing the hundreds of yards of guttering on the house and stables.

George arrived at nine o'clock and in his dogged way began at once to clear the overgrown brush around the cottage and add it to the growing pile in the paddock. Since it was Tuesday Charlie was late.

Slowly the mist dispersed and a pale winter sun broke through. By 11.30 my little team was complete. It turned into a beautiful winter day, the ground still hard from the frost, the air crisp and clear but the sun sufficiently warm to make a jacket unnecessary. The fine weather seemed to lift the men's spirits and there was a bustle of activity around the house. By midday, a thin curl of blue smoke rose from George's bonfire in the pad-dock, Charlie was purposefully digging a trench to form the footings of the retaining wall for the septic tank, his blue fisher-man's balaclava bobbing up and down below the level of the forecourt as he worked. I could hear monosyllabic instructions coming through the open window of the new bathroom as the pink T-shirt continued rubbing down, and Graham's early Elvis Presley medley floated on the still air from the stable yard, as he attempted to repair the cracked, cast-iron guttering with some unused lengths, which we had found in the top stable.

I made coffee for the boys and sat in the sun on the stone steps outside the garden door at the end of the passage, holding the warm mug in my hands and looking down past the newly shorn viburnum, across the tennis court to the gently rising hill of the field beyond. In the nut walk, Leroy disturbed a mallard on the tail water and it flew, squawking indignantly, past the front of the house to the safety of the mill pond.

I finished my coffee and went back into the house. Roger was standing by the kitchen table. He handed me a business card.

'This chap dropped by on Saturday. He said he knew the Mill and he'd seen all the works that were going on and wondered what was happening.'

I read the card:

> Colin Ridgewell and Son
> Landscape Design and Implementation
> Local Authority approved contractors

I remembered him at once from when I was ten. A well-built young man in his twenties with a thick mane of tawny-coloured hair who lived with his mother in a cottage at the top of the lane. He used to come down to the fields in the evenings and at weekends with his two white ferrets, Percy and Millicent, in a sack, and he would take me with him as he knelt in the grass and sent the ferrets down after rabbits. He would let me hold the ferrets as he made his preparations, netting off all the other exits of the rabbit warren. I used to love holding the warm, excited little animals with their pungent smell, sharp, white teeth and inquisitive noses. They would climb into my open aertex shirt and go exploring round my back, making me laugh as they tickled my rib cage, before burrowing down past my waist band and emerging from the bottom of my shorts.

Somehow Colin never quite succeeded in netting off all the exits from the warren and time and again, after he had sent Percy and Millicent down the hole, a family of bunnies would emerge from a hole by the hedge ten yards away, lollop unconcernedly along it and disappear into a different warren, while Colin knelt, staring fixedly at his original hole and calling words of encouragement to his team.

Once they were down a rabbit hole, Percy and Millicent showed little interest in coming back and I could see their point of view. There they were in a nice warm burrow, full of interesting smells. They might have made a kill and were lying curled up in a furry ball, sleeping off what Colin had intended to be his dinner. If they came out, they would be grabbed by the scruff of the neck, stuffed into an old sack and carried, jolting, over

Colin's shoulder as he cycled back up the hill to his mother's cottage. There, they would be put in a draughty, straw-lined wooden pen outside the back door and kept underfed to make them eager for the next outing. I often wondered who was exploiting who, as I knelt there loyally while the day wore on and Colin whistled and called and made rurr-rurring noises until dusk began to fall and Lucy's head would appear over the top of the straggling hedge on the house side of the river, by the tall, walnut tree and she would call out, 'Come on, Charles, it's time for tea.'

I picked up the telephone and called the Hedingham number.

'Good heavens, Charles! I haven't spoken to you for a good while.'

'It's been a couple of years.' I replied with the insouciance I had acquired from Lawrence Parsons.

'What are you up to down at the Mill?'

'I'm making some alterations. You're doing landscaping now.'

'Yes, we've been doing it for a good many years now, me and Robert, my son.'

'I'm turning the front garden into a gravelled forecourt and parking area. Would you be interested in coming over and giving me an estimate?'

'I'd be happy to. It would be nice to work at the old place. I can come on Friday morning. Would that suit you?'

'Yes, that would be fine. Don't forget the ferrets.'

He laughed. 'Ah, you remember them do you? Yes, I used to do a fair bit of shooting with your father as well, and with your grandfather, Colonel Warrens. Your father used to like me to bring my dogs, Punch and Judy. They put up a fair bit of game. I remember one day, we were down in the willows and my two dogs were chasing a rabbit. They were close up behind it, as it zig-zagged across an open stretch of grass. To my horror, I heard a gun go off, over my left shoulder. It was your father. He let off both barrels. Fortunately he didn't hit anything. Then he turned to me and said, "I must be getting old, Colin. I missed the rabbit and both the dogs." They were good times in Nutleam. I was pleased to have known your father.'

*

The next day, 4 February, was the day of the skip and February 3rd had disappeared due to my inability to see the tiny date inset on the face of my watch. In February 1992, which was a leap year, it had lost touch with the Gregorian calendar and lacking the technical expertise to alter it, I had continued with it as it was, making allowances on a month to month basis, so that on 1 March, I added two days, in April remain the same, in May add one day and so on. These calculations only applied of course on days when I could find my glasses. Otherwise I remained blissfully unaware of the date, unless I asked my daughter Juliet, who always seemed to know because of her school activities.

Yesterday when I looked at it spectacleless, it seemed to say 2nd February. Adding on my carried-forward figure of one day for the last eleven months should have given me a true date of 3rd February. This morning when I made out a cheque in the bank, they insisted that it was 4th February.

Over the days I had made a habit of picking up all the bits of metal, redundant machinery and unburnable rubbish that lay in the chicken run, the stables, the garages, the cart lodge and in odd places around the paddocks and dropping them in a pile in the stable yard, intending eventually to order a skip to cart them away, having given up all hope of a totter. Totters didn't seem to exist any more. None came down the lane, as they used to, and the *Essex Chronicle* carried no advertisements asking for scrap metal. Today was the day the skip would be delivered.

Len was late, working on his other job. Charlie and George were happily at work in the forecourt with the cement-mixer, laying the foundations for the wall to the septic tank. I waited by the pile of metal in the stable yard for the skip to be delivered at 11 o'clock, like an anxious groom waiting at the altar. By lunchtime it had not arrived and I began to wonder if the driver was having problems with the date inset on his watch.

Finally, at two o'clock it came. Charlie, having appraised my pile of jumbled metal with a professional eye, had advised me to order 'a four yarder'. When it arrived it looked hopelessly inadequate to consume my twisted collection of iron.

'It's all in the packing, Chas,' Charlie said helpfully, wandering back down the lane from the stable yard to the cement-mixer and leaving me to get on with it. I had visions of professional skip-packers, travelling the country, helping untutored householders dispose of their rubbish. Would they be listed in the *Yellow Pages*? Perhaps the AA could help?

There was no time to enlist professional assistance. The skip had to be collected again at four o'clock. Reluctantly, I set to work on my own. Since the lorry was too large to get through the double-leaf doors of the stable yard, the driver had left the skip on the other side of the lane, on the triangle of land which would form Bob and Vally's front garden. This was my first mistake, since every journey from the pile to the skip involved crossing the lane twice. I picked up my first item, a large, heavy oil drum, carried it to the door, stopped for a blue Fiesta to pass, dropped it in the skip, stopped for a white van to pass, returned to the pile; picked up two lengths of broken, cast-iron guttering, waited for a green Vauxhall and dropped them in the skip, waited for the Black Nutleam Hospital ambulance to pass and returned to the pile.

I began to take a keen interest in the objects I was carrying. A tyre from the grey-blue sunbeam Alpine which my father had bought in 1960. He, who never willingly changed anything, had driven off to London one morning in a black Austin A40 and returned in the evening in the low-slung two seater. As if this moment of uncharacteristic madness were not enough, the reason for his purchase was even more startling. Not for him the traditional justification for a car purchase: 'It does nought to 60 in eight seconds. It has a two-litre engine and 185 brake horsepower. I can get 27 miles to the gallon.'

None of these technical considerations were of interest to my father. When I asked him why he had bought it, he said, 'I liked the colour.'

The A40, in which he had departed, was the family car. It had four doors, which was useful when my mother and we three children had to make a journey together. Since, by this time, we were in our mid-teens and almost fully grown, journeys in the Alpine were a nightmare, as two of us had to sit on the cramped, rear parcel shelf with our knees pressing against the backs of the seats in front and our heads bent forward to get under the low roof. I had semi-permanent backache in my teens, until Anne and Juliet left home and I graduated to the front seat.

A large, metal oil drum, sealed fast and unbelievably heavy with some unknown liquid. I rolled it over the lane and lifted it into the skip, praying that it would not be dumped near a river and the contents seep out, poisoning half the wildlife of East Anglia.

A bent and rusting Huntley & Palmers biscuit tin, in which Lucy used to keep her homemade sponge cakes, which she would bring out of the larder at teatime.

A misshapen, metal sieve with a wooden surround with which Bearman used to sift ashes from the Aga, before scattering the fine ash dust on the vegetable garden, leaving the lumps in an ever-increasing pile by the stable yard door, until it was so large that he couldn't get his wheelbarrow past it. Rather than move it, he took to wheeling his barrow down the lane and into the garden by the front gate, having by that time developed acute Millitis.

The skip was filling rapidly but the pile did not seem to be diminishing to the same extent. Perhaps Charlie was right. I decided to concentrate on my packing and maximize the space in the skip by putting small items into larger containers before dropping them in the skip. Dutifully, I located a square metal box. I put a broken drain grill in the bottom. I filled a paint tin with short lengths of snapped iron fencing stakes and put the tin in the box. I coiled a length of lead-encased electric cable round the other objects in the box and filled in the gaps with rusty gate hinges. I looked at the finished result. It was certainly neatly packed and would only take up a small amount of space in the skip. Thinking that Charlie would be pleased with me, I bent over and picked up the box by its sides. The bottom fell out.

While I considered my future policy in the light of this set-back, I picked up a bale of rusty chicken wire, dragged it to the lane and waited for a large, blue van. When it had passed, I dragged the bale across the lane, not noticing a white Honda coming rapidly round the Mill corner. As I dragged the cumbersome wire manfully across the lane, I didn't notice the inside uncoiling behind me. Suddenly my forward progress was halted as the wheels of the Honda drove over the trailing wire and then was abruptly restarted as it passed, throwing me into the muddy verge of the lane and thrusting my face into the branches of a young elder tree growing in the spot that was destined to become Bob and Vally's front door.

By four o'clock the skip was full. There was no discernible difference in the size of my pile. Morosely, I retired to the kitchen and made tea for the boys. George stood immaculate amidst piles of cement, sand, ballast and lime, his crease intact, his trousers spotless. I looked like Worzel Gummidge.

On Monday I would graduate to an eight-yarder.

Next morning, Colin Ridgewell arrived at 10.15 with his tall, fair-haired son, Robert. Now 61, he had filled out and his mane of hair had thinned but he was instantly recognizable as the ferret-master of 40 years before. He greeted me with a long, slow smile and a warm, firm handshake as they stood on the hard standing, looking at the Mill.

'It's been a while since I worked in the Mill as a lad. I was only allowed on the ground floor, you know. They had strict rules then. Otherwise I'd back the horse and cart up below that door on the first floor and Dick Weller would drop the sacks of corn into the cart so accurate that I'd never have to move 'em.'

'I remember him quite well.'

'Yes, I expect you do. He was a tough old boy. As you know he used to live next to us at the top of the lane. I remember one day after he retired, he was doing some work in his shed and hit his thumb with a club hammer. He came round to me, I must have been about 17 at the time, and said, "Can you give me a hand with this, Colin," showing me his thumb. He'd crushed the end, so that the flesh was spread out around the nail. It was a helluva mess. I said, "I can't do anything with that, Dick, but I'll walk up to the hospital with you." Of course, there were no cars in those days. "No, no," he said, "I can't be bothering with that. You do it. Just trim it up, I'll see you all right boy." He didn't want to come into the house or even sit down, so he stood in the doorway while I trimmed the loose flesh off with a razor. For the next two weeks he came to the door each morning and I dressed his thumb and after the treatment was finished, he gave me half an ounce of tobacco.'

Colin had an even, deliberate way of speaking which was emphasized by the rich timbre of his voice, but it wasn't garrulousness. I knew for certain at the outset that the speech would end when its message had been imparted. There was a careful and satisfying roundness about its delivery and I thought how good he would have been as a radio commentator.

I led them round into the forecourt, showing them where the trenches had been dug and where the septic tank had been installed. Colin asked where the tank was going to drain, in order to work out the grading falls of the area he was to gravel.

'It flows out into the river,' I said, 'it's been approved by the National Rivers Authority. Binders, the septic tank experts who installed it, claim that the effluent is so pure after it's been through the treatment plant, that you can drink it. Not that I'd want to try it.'

Colin laughed. 'Well, over in that field there,' he said pointing across the river, 'on what was Ossie Claricoat's field, there used to be a treatment plant for Black Nutleam Hospital, or sanitarium, as it was then. The old boy that looked after it, Hutley, or Puddin' Hutley, as he was known, used to say to us boys that you could drink the effluent from that plant. He had an old, blue, enamel mug and just to prove the point, he used to drink some himself. This, mind you, was effluent from a TB Hospital.'

'What age was he when he died?' I asked sceptically.

'Oh, he was over 90. It never did him any harm. They used to say he needed a step ladder to pick the Brussels sprouts he grew around that treatment plant. He used to sell them in Banktree market as cabbages.'

As we walked up to the stable yard to show Colin the water main trenches, which I would want him to tamp down and regravel so that they tied in with the new forecourt, he noticed the entwined copper bracelet that I wore on my right wrist. My mother had given it to me when I was at university and had experienced the first twinges of rheumatism.

'What's that, Charles?' He pointed at the bracelet.

'It's copper. It's supposed to ease rheumatism.'

'One of Dick Weller's three Rs.'

'What do you mean?'

'Dick used to tell the weather by the three Rs. Rooks, rabbits and rheumatism. If the rabbits were feeding between 12 and two o'clock, it would rain within two hours. If the rooks flew into the rookery in the morning, it would rain in the afternoon and, if he had a twinge of rheumatism, it would rain tomorrow. And very accurate he was, a lot better than the weather man and it was important information for a miller to have, seeing as he had to control the level of the river, so as it didn't flood the lane.'

We returned to the forecourt and Colin and Robert took measurements, measured falls and considered the best way to achieve what I was looking for. By lunchtime they were finished.

'All right, Charles. I think we've got the picture. If you can just give us a couple of days, we'll work out the price and put it in a letter to you. I hope we'll be successful in getting the job. It would be nice to work at the old Mill again.'

They drove off, waving cheerfully in their red Mazda van and I went back into the house. Colin's parting remark indicated that he assumed I would be getting some competitive estimates to compare his price. I knew I wouldn't bother. There was never any doubt that he was going to do this job, with loving care, attention to detail, and at the lowest price his affection would permit. I looked forward to the day they would start.

I spent the afternoon tidying up. Clearing up the stable yard and the chicken run, collecting all the tools which I and the others had used during the week and putting them neatly in the woodshed, so that they could be dispersed again the following week. Piling up the loose bricks and half-bricks, which Charlie had left around the septic tank, no doubt as part of some strategic plan to which he would return, frustrated by my neatness, on Monday. I returned to the Mill the hand tools and lengths of wood, which we had borrowed from Len and Simon during the week, and finally tidied up my bedroom and the paper-strewn table in the dining-room, which I used as my desk.

Carrying out any simple job at Fulford Mill involved an inordinate amount of walking. After the long week, the cold, the snatched meals, and my battle with the skip, by four o'clock I felt unbearably weary. I picked up my toilet bag from the corridor, where Len had left it, threw my filthy jeans, shirt and sweater into my case and drove slowly back to Surrey, through the gathering gloom and the Friday night traffic.

There was a nine-mile hold-up at the Dartford Crossing where a lorry had shed its load and I finally arrived home at nine o'clock, after Juliet and Edward had gone to bed and too late for supper. Sympathetically, Annette offered me eggs and bacon, but my consciousness had gone into free fall and I opted for a long, hot bath instead. Finally, I climbed into bed and lay prostrate in the cool, fresh sheets, watching the fat, brown spider, which lived in the oak beam by the window, telepathically sending him a message of greeting from his cousins at Fulford Mill. Annette slipped into bed beside me and surveyed my unshaven face.

'Do you know your beard is almost completely white?'

'Oh, does it make me look like George C Scott or Ernest Hemingway?' I asked, fishing for a compliment to round off the week. She raised herself on her elbow and looked thoughtfully down into my face.

'No,' she said, after a moment's consideration. 'It makes you look like Compo.'

I smiled, my eyelids drooped, sleep washed over me.

Chapter Six

There was a lot to be done at Fulford Mill, co-ordinating my team and organizing the supplies which they needed, so I sorted out my own office work at home over the weekend and drove down late on Sunday night.

Roger greeted me at breakfast next morning. 'Ah, our man from Surrey.'

'Our man from Essex you mean. I'm at home so rarely that Annette and the children have forgotten who I am.'

'Quite right too. The male's only role is to provide territory.'

'What do you mean?'

'Well, it's the relationship between men and women.'

As I ate my Weetabix, I learned that this is basically territorial.

'The male's only role is to provide sufficient territory for the female or females, depending on how successful he is, to rear the young. You can see this most obviously in lions, where the male patrols the boundary of his territory and frightens off competing males. The bigger the territory he can guard, the more females he can support.'

'What about providing food?' I asked, spreading Olde English marmalade on my toast.

'No, that's not part of the male's biological role. He may join in the hunt and in some species, particularly birds, he may assist in bringing food to the nest, but it is more as a bit of fun, than his primary role. How often do you go to the supermarket?'

'Now and again.'

'Exactly, it's a bit of fun, but Annette goes all the time. No, females are biologically the providers. It is as if the male has said, "Here's your bit of territory, now get on with it." In lion hunts, it is the lionesses who do all the work and you see this reflected in early man and some agrarian societies. The man may go off as a hunter with his spear and come back after three days with a deer over his shoulder, all very heroic, but in the mean-time the female has been feeding the family on flour-based foods and vegetables, which provide 90 per cent of the essential vita-mins and nutrients. The male offering, while being dense pro-tein, is really only the equivalent of bringing occasional sweets.'

Illusions about love and romance, commitment, sharing and life partnership disappeared through the half-open kitchen door, but I knew what he meant. Whenever I'd embarked on a partic-ularly perilous and uncertain commercial adventure, I had felt that I was patrolling the very limits of my territory and creditors, liquidators, receivers and the Trustee in Bankruptcy were preda-tors, prowling in the shadows beyond my frontiers, waiting to make incursions into my domain and threaten the equilibrium of my brood.

They in their turn seemed to have little need for me to partici-pate in their cub-like romps, preferring to visualize me on the horizon, barking at bank managers and raising my hackles to the Inland Revenue.

I had often smiled in reflection at the solitariness of the male role and the curious bonding that took place with competing males as we skirted around some invisible commercial bound-ary, setting down scent markers and advancing and retreating in negotiation.

It was always illuminating to hear our innermost instincts unravelled by Roger's acute biological perception, however politically incorrect and however disillusioning the experience.

I had ordered another skip, an eight yarder this time and it arrived at ten o'clock. Charlie and George were at work with the cement-mixer. I complimented Charlie on his shocking pink, Andre Agassi tennis cap and noted the dangerous crease in George's dark blue trousers, as I walked up to the stable yard once again, to fill the skip. Remembering the hazards of crossing the lane, I used the old pram in which Lucy had wheeled Anne, Juliet and myself when we were babies, to ferry my lumps of metal and rubbish across the lane. It was on its last legs and, being highly sprung, it bounced up and down alarmingly as I wheeled an old washing machine, a 25-gallon oil drum, the broken cast-iron baths, which had been used as watering troughs in the paddocks, and rolls of barbed wire, across the lane.

Bearman's drainage-pipe rose supports were too heavy for me to lift on my own and I enlisted George's assistance in carrying them across the road. He helped me tidy up the remaining pieces and packed them into the bulging skip with exemplary neatness. He obviously had a City & Guilds in skip-packing. As he walked back down the lane, I was delighted to see a smudge of cement dust on his trousers.

I stood looking at the pram and wondering whether I should throw it on the skip. It looked ready to go and meet its maker, but it had sentimental value and possibly might have financial value as well.

When I was 19, I had used the money that I had saved up from my various holiday jobs and, for £70, had bought a 1938 MGVA. It was a big, blue cabriolet tourer, with blue leather seats, copper pipes instead of hoses under the bonnet, stainless steel spokes and running boards. For two years it had been my pride and joy until I finished my degree at Cambridge and was about to emigrate to America. I reasoned that since I didn't know if or when I would be back, it would be better that someone else should look after it and enjoy it, rather than that it should lie deteriorating in one of our damp, bird-infested garages and I'd sold it to Peter Hines for a nominal sum. Reading through a classic car magazine recently, I was interested to see that it was now worth rather more than my BMW. All that swapping and changing of cars over the years, in search of improved specification, more power and greater comfort when I could have been driving around in a car with real style that was also an investment.

Perhaps the pram was the MGVA of the baby carriage world and collectors were scouring the country for examples of that vintage. But perhaps too that was exactly the attitude that had lead to Fulford Mill becoming a hotch-potch of broken and defunct memorabilia; but then again did that matter? I had always been amazed, in the early days of clearing the house, when I had filled the plastic fertilizer sacks from the top stable with completely useless bit of rusting and broken fencing stakes, iron buckets with holes in the bottom and no handles and empty paint pots, and taken them to the council tip in Witham, how other people at the tip would scour my offerings as I left. Men in anoraks and brown corduroy trousers would pick up a length of jagged metal and stand inspecting it with the intensity of Arthur Negus examining an eighteenth-century silver candlestick by Paul Storr.

I had read in a newspaper article that car boot sales were the fasting growing form of outdoor recreation in England. Such is the jackdaw nature of human beings, that I could readily see that it was about to be followed by the sport of recycling.

I was in a dither of indecision, as I stood in the lane, first wheeling the pram to the skip to discard it and then wheeling it back to the stable yard to preserve it. This was useless. Time was passing. Finally, it dawned on me. I picked the pram up and placed it resolutely and prominently on top of the skip. If anyone was qualified to ascertain if it had any intrinsic value or future use, it was the connoisseurs of Albaton council tip.

I had a meeting scheduled for three o'clock with Richard Shaw, the senior partner of R J Shaw & Co, the firm of solicitors in Banktree, which handled the legal administration of my father's estate. Strutt & Parker had received an offer to purchase the cottage and I needed to agree the boundaries of the land which would be sold with the cottage, in order to establish whether an easement would be necessary for the passage of water, since the old metal water main, which carried the supply across the top of our paddocks to Fulford Farm on the corner of the lane, passed close to the cottage.

After lunch I got into the car. It wouldn't start. I was shocked. However uninspiring my car might have been as a fashion statement, however basic its specification and however functional its cloth interior trim, at least it had a comforting, Teutonic reliability. I lifted the bonnet and stood looking, with uncomprehending eyes, at the gleaming mass of technology that filled the engine compartment. There was almost nothing that I recognized from my years of lying under the family cars with Bearman or my own old bangers with Denis Parsons, while oil from the sump and gearbox dribbled on to our arms and faces, as we changed piston-rings and renewed crankshafts.

This was a robot from an alien planet. Blue, plastic hoses ran in a neat, clipped loom from black, circular cylinders by the driver's compartment, down into a solid slab of alloy in the centre. Square, plastic boxes in white and yellow stood precisely above the wheel arches, with blue cables running purposefully into an oblong, titanium case butting on to the alloy. Each container had a neat sticker of instructions on the outside, but they were all in German and ended with an exclamation mark. There were no comforting spark plugs, no carburettor, no distributor and it was all so clean. How could any engine so clean possibly work?

Len and Simon joined me from the Mill. Charlie and George abandoned the cement-mixer. David poked an inquisitive nose out of the top floor of the Granary, where he was constructing a bedroom window. Finally, Roger ambled across the lane from the office, abandoning an aminated discussion with the Natural History department of the BBC.

There was much drawing in of breath, sucking of teeth and pursing of lips as seven grown men with a combined age of 318 years, considered this technological challenge. After ten minutes of deliberation, three centuries of experience were distilled into Charlie's succinct advice: 'I should try it again, Chas.'

I got in and turned the key. The car started at once. Reflecting on the irreplaceable value of experience, I drove into Banktree and parked in R J Shaw & Co's car park. Concerned about starting the car again, I left it running while I walked to Sainsbury's for my shopping and then returned for my meeting with Richard.

Another alumnus of St Margaret's, he had taken over the practice from his father, who had frequently instructed my own father on local cases. A tall man with a pencil moustache and a gold Parker pen, little changed from the days when, as clumsy 12-year-olds, we had attended dancing classes together in the Old Conservative Club, he sat patiently behind his desk, as I perused the scale plan. I had forgotten my glasses, but I found that if I held the plan with my arms outstretched at the very furthest extent of my fingers, the squiggly lines of the boundaries came into focus. Unfortunately, the main source of light in the room came from the large french window, giving on to the car park and in order for this to fall on the plan, I had to hold it over the desk.

'No, no, don't worry,' Richard sighed politely, privately wanting to shoot me, as I held the plan inches from his face. For reasons of myopia, the meeting took longer than I had envisaged, but finally we were agreed on the boundaries of the curtilage and I walked back to the car. It had run out of petrol.

The next morning was bitterly cold and a fine drizzle of sleet swept in from the north. Roger's theme for the day was the interaction of social, religious and economic history. Over a bowl of muesli he set out his opening position with a review of the grant of the manor of Crossing, including the site of Fulford Mill, to the Brothers of the Knighthood of Solomon's Temple at Jerusalem, the Knights Templar, by Queen Maud in 1137. I learned that this was an arrangement of administrative convenience.

As I listened, I pondered my footwear for the day. In view of the extreme cold, I decided on my thick, outdoor socks, since I wanted to start clearing up the brick rubble in the stable yard. George telephoned at nine o'clock to say that he'd had a look outside his front door and decided that it was a day for younger men. Charlie arrived, sporting a leather airman's cap with ear flaps as protection against the weather.

'It's a bit nippy, Chas. I think I'll cut up those lengths of wood in one of the stables.'

We went up to the stable yard and Charlie disappeared into one of the stables, while I began to separate out the half-bricks and rubble, stacking the bricks against the wall and dumping the rubble by the new gate, from where it could easily be barrowed down to the front of the house, as hard core for the forecourt. I had hardly begun, when Roger called from the kitchen door:

'Phone, Charles. It's Richard Shaw.'

I went back to the kitchen and took off my boots. They were tight because of my thick socks and I had to hold the doorjambs with both hands and pull with the heel against the doorstep, until they would come off. Finally, after a three-minute struggle they were off and I went through to the phone in the living-room. Richard had rung off, unaware of the valiant efforts which were being made to speak to him. I rang him back. He'd gone out.

I hung up, went back to the kitchen, pulled on my boots, walked up to the yard, put on my work gloves and started at the bricks and rubble again. Charlie called out from the stable, 'Can you go up to Beta Builders, Chas? I need some more four by one.'

Rather than take my boots off again, I got into the car in my wellingtons. I found that my boots were so wide that they pressed the accelerator and the brake at the same time. I went back to the kitchen door and went through the three-minute struggle again. I noticed that it took four minutes. I found my shoes, but couldn't get them on over the thick socks. I took off the thick socks and put on my thin, indoor socks and drove up to Beta Builders. Paul was having an interview with the senior regional VAT inspector. Ted took my order. 'We'll drop 'em down this afternoon, Chas.'

I returned to the house, pulled off my thin socks, put on my thick socks and boots and returned to the yard. Charlie stood in the shelter of the overhang above the hayloft.

'I'll be needing two nine-foot lengths, Chas.'

'Where do we get them from?'

'You'll have to go to Nordic Timber at Silver End. They'll deliver.'

'Can't it wait until tomorrow?'

'Not really.'

I went back to the house and embarked wearily on the boot ritual. It took six minutes and was interspersed with rest periods. I put on my thin socks and shoes and drove over to Golden Tye. I couldn't find Nordic Timber and stopped alongside a pedestrian, hurrying along the pavement in an overcoat and flat-cap against the gusting sleet.

'Excuse me, can you tell me where Nordic Timber is?'

He stopped and looked in the car window. 'Hello, Charles. Yes, it's on the Bradwell Road, about 50 yards after the turning on the left.'

'Who are you?' I asked, astonished that he knew my name.

'I'm Ted Roberts. You used to drink up at the Fox.'

'Oh yes,' I said, not remembering him. We chatted for a few minutes about the changes in Silver End and the old Crittall factory and then I followed his directions to Nordic Timber. I hadn't been in the Fox for at least 25 years and I wondered what dreadful indiscretion I had committed for him to have remembered my greatly changed face after a quarter of a century.

Praying that I'd never meet him in a police line-up, I ordered the nine-foot lengths and drove back to the house. Doggedly I exchanged my thin socks for my thick socks and my shoes for my boots and returned to the stable yard. The pile of half-bricks and rubble had grown. Charlie had taken advantage of my absence and a brief lull in the sleet to break up the short section of wall, which had run at right angles to the fence and had thoughtfully deposited the debris in my work area. I bent to restart my sifting and Roger's face appeared at the gate.

'Oh, Charles, I was just wondering if you could get some sandwiches for lunch. I know it's my turn, but I'm expecting a call from my agent and I can't go out.'

I walked back to the house with him and set to work with the doorjambs and the doorstep. Roger continued with his socio-economic thesis and I learned that the Knights Templar were founded in the eleven hundreds to protect travellers to the holy sites of Christ's birth and crucifixion against the Muslims and

Saracens. They built large forts, run by noblemen and monks all the way across the Christian world to the Holy Land. Because they were an international order of monks with military strength, traders began to entrust their money to them for transmission across Europe and they became bankers.

At last my boots were off. The original three minutes had stretched to seven. My back ached. I was panting. I put on my thin socks and my shoes and drove up to Nutleam Stores. I returned and sat groaning at the kitchen table, nibbling desultorily at my ham and sweet-pickle sandwich.

I discovered that Philip the Fair of France became alarmed at the growth in wealth and power being accumulated by the Knights Templar and discredited them by broadcasting the dubious rumour that they worshipped cats. In conjunction with Pope Clement V, he arranged for a bill of suppression to be read out at a public ceremony in Avignon in 1312 and in 1314 all the Templar lands passed into the hands of the Order of the Hospital of St John the Baptist at Jerusalem, or the Hospitallers as they were known. Like the Templars they were dedicated Christian soldiers, but their vows required them to put their healing duties before their military ones.

'This was the beginning of the National Health Service,' Roger remarked. As he embarked on a diversion on the subject of health management during the six centuries between the Hospitallers in 1314 and Beveridge in 1945, I reviewed my footwear policy for the afternoon. I was clearly weakening and I doubted if I would have the strength to get my boots off again. I was determined to achieve something during the day and decided to brave the freezing conditions and keep my thin socks on.

The afternoon was blissfully uninterrupted. The sleet lifted but it became, if anything, even colder. By four o'clock, I had a neat pile of bricks stacked against the wall and a pile of rubble by the gate. I had lost all feeling in my feet.

I went back to the house and slipped off my boots. My back ached, my knees ached, my legs ended at the ankles. I went upstairs to the bathroom. Len had left for the day and I ran a bath, anticipating the luxury of sinking into the soothing water as I hastily undressed. I stepped into the bath and lay back with relief. After 15 seconds my feet began to throb. In 30 seconds they were burning like hot coals. I leapt out of the bath, vaguely remembering something that Lucy had said about not putting cold feet into hot water. I think I had dismissed it, with the wisdom of a 12-year-old, as an old wive's tale.

My feet were too painful to stand on. I hopped from one foot to the other on the bare, hardboard floor, with its thin film of plaster dust, exclaiming, 'Oh, aah, aah, ouch, ooh!' I was leaving dark, wet footprints in the dusty surface, like instructions for the rumba on the floor of an Arthur Murray dance studio. I began to jog on the spot. Roger's voice wafted up from the scullery beneath me:

'Is that some traditional Welsh dance, Charles?'

I ignored him. The circulation was returning to my feet and I climbed back into the bath. My feet did not complain. I lay back and closed my eyes, letting the hot water soothe my aching bones. After 20 minutes' relaxation, my mind turned to the idea of washing. I looked for the soap. It was absent and I realized that this was one of those days when Len, in his meticulous way, had cleared the bathroom of all extraneous clutter, while he got on with his decorating and had left me soapless. I got out of the bath and, naked, went in search of it. I finally located it at the bottom of the airing cupboard, stuck to a 1959 edition of the *Essex Chronicle*, which lined the floor. Carefully, I prised it loose, but part of the newspaper came with it. Thankfully, I climbed back into the bath and read an interesting account of a burglary in Southend in 1959, which had stuck to the Lifebuoy.

'Yes, what I was trying to tell you, when we were interrupted yesterday,' Roger said at breakfast next morning, 'was that Queen Maud, or Queen Matilda as she was known, was given the Manor of Crossing by her uncle, Count Eustace of Boulogne. He had been granted it by William The Conqueror, in return for his assistance in the invasion of England in 1066. William had confiscated it from Harold, Earl of Essex, after his defeat and death at the Battle of Hastings.'

'What, King Harold?'

'Yes.'

'He with the arrow in the eye?'

'The same.'

'So he owned the manor of Crossing, including Fulford Mill?'

'Yes. Of course, it wasn't the same mill building, as you know, but there was a mill on the site. William had an inventory carried out of all the land and buildings in England which had fallen under his control and incorporated it into the Domesday Book in 1086. This shows that the manor of Crossing contained five mills, of which this was one. It was known as Fulfan Mill.'

In order to create a head of water to turn the millwheel, the river had been diverted from its natural course and a straight reach, 300 yards long, had been dug, taking the water in a direct line to the Mill and raising the banks above the level of the surrounding fields. It was strange to think that the stretch of water, where I had paddled my triangular, homemade plywood boat at the age of ten, had been constructed by hand a thousand years before.

After breakfast I couldn't start my car. Not trusting the accumulated wisdom of the Fulford ensemble, I called out the AA. An angular and enthusiastic young man called Wayne got it running in no time, but said the problem was the injectors and I would have to have them checked at the main BMW garage in Bishop's Stortford.

I drove the 15 miles to the Hertfordshire town and found the garage on the bypass. It was a long, low, modern building with smoked-glass windows and a huge car park, packed with gleaming vehicles. It looked like a modern hospital in Dusseldorf. There was an opulent hush in the fashionably carpeted reception hall. Immaculately tailored and coiffed young women looked up from their computer terminals as I entered, and paused with long, pink fingernails hovering over their keyboards, as they surveyed my unshaven face and dishevelled appearance. The Fulford uniform was obviously considered demode in this outpost of the fatherland.

A young man in a dark grey business suit with thin red stripes wafted silently towards me carrying a mobile phone.

'Can we be of assistance, sir?' he murmured in cultured tones. Noticing that his thumb was hovering over the panic button, I quickly explained my problem.

'Perhaps if you could drive the car into the operating bay, sir, then we'll carry out a diagnosis.'

I drove the car round to the side of the building and a young houseman in a three-quarter-length white coat came across the spotless, blue-tiled floor.

'We'll take it from here, sir. Perhaps you'd like a coffee in the lounge while you wait?'

'I'd rather watch,' I said, fearing the manicured disdain of the 'lounge'.

'Very well, sir. I know some people are anxious.'

He drove the car into the operating bay and fitted terminals from his diagnostic machine to the gleaming alloy under the bonnet. His senior, a consultant, aged approximately 22, attached a stethoscope from around his neck to the titanium case. Exclamation marks were no deterrent to him. He bent forward with an expression of intense concentration on his face as the engine idled. After a few seconds he took off his stethoscope and examined the green, liquid crystal read out on the body scanner. He came towards me with a calm but concerned expression. I had to admire his bedside manner.

'I'm afraid there's no doubt about it, sir. It needs a new set of injectors.'

'How much will that cost?'

He mentioned a figure that would have paid for a complete heart and liver transplant.

'They'll be ready tomorrow, sir. It's quite a quick operation.' I wondered if I could get cover under BUPA.

Thursday was the anniversary of my father's birthday. Roger's thesis for the day was the connection between our respective academic disciplines.

'All economic activity is basically biological,' he pronounced

provocatively. At that moment, however, the doorbell rang and
M & N Electricians arrived to examine the jumble of brown electrical cables, which looked like overcooked spaghetti on the end
wall of the landing. The mains supply entered the house at this
point and the junction and fuse boxes would have to be moved
when the new window was put in. I suspended my education as
I accompanied Mick and Nick upstairs. They took one look at
the ageing installation and turned to me glumly:

'Can't be moved I'm afraid,' said Mick or Nick.

'Why's that?'

'It's rubber cabling. They passed a new law in January and we
can't make alterations which still connect to a rubber-cased circuit,' said Nick or Mick.

'So what can we do?'

'All we can do is rewire the house.'

David Forrest was scheduled to arrive at eleven to view the
progress on the house and I decided to ask his advice about this
unexpected addition to the programme. I was particularly anxious to show him the bathroom. In common with most estate
agents he thought that kitchens and bathrooms were crucial in
selling a house. Since turning the three rooms, which served as a
food preparation area, into a modern housewife's delight would
have entailed an investment which could be better used in resur-
facing the M25, I hoped that the new bathroom would go some
way to rekindling his enthusiasm.

He arrived on time and I took him in through the front door.
Although the forecourt was not yet graded and gravelled he
commented at once on what an improvement it was, in presenting the house in a coherent way. I was encouraged, as I led him
up the stairs. We paused on the landing where the window was
destined to go and I explained about the electrical problems.

'Is it worth going to the expense of rewiring the house?'

'Yes it is. You'll be taking away another problem in the eyes of
a prospective purchaser and, anyway, I don't see that you've got
much choice.'

Nervously, I led him through the old bathroom and the small
landing to the new bathroom. It still had a bare hardboard floor,

but the decoration was almost complete and I felt it was a bright and airy room, with two windows looking out over the court-yard and to the garden beyond.

'It's a good-sized family bathroom,' I said encouragingly.

'Mmm,' he murmured.

'I would think that a mother with a young family would appreciate it,' I pressed.

He wandered silently round the room, noting the layout. He seemed unimpressed. I began to get anxious. Was my father right and I didn't know anything about building? Was the bath in the wrong place? Were the units the wrong colour? I led him out on to the landing.

'And out here there will be a large airing cupboard.'

Silence.

'It would be very useful,' I added pathetically.

He wandered back into the bathroom and sat down on the toi-let, his face expressionless, as he looked out of the window.

'Ah! I can sit here and look out of the window and see if the gardener is late. Now that appeals to me.'

He approved.

We progressed out into the garden and David surveyed the new fencing and the gate to the stable yard where the potting shed had been. Charlie was busy constructing a wooden cover-ing for the septic tank. My idea was that not only would it dis-guise the tank, but future owners could put garden furniture on it and use it as a patio, since it caught the evening sun in the summer and looked down over the mill pool.

'It's coming along quite well,' David commented as we walked up the lane to his car. 'We should be able to start mar-keting again in the spring. Tell me, is that chap by the septic tank one of the contractor's men or one of yours?'

'That's Charlie. He's one of mine.'

'I like the stetson.'

As he drove off, Bob Hudson's face appeared at the door on the first floor of the Granary overlooking the lane. Two tall and serious-looking men in their thirties, dressed in grey overalls, stood behind him.

'Hello, Charles, would you like to meet these two reprobates?'

I climbed up the wall ladder to the first floor and Bob introduced us.

'This is David Andrews from the Crossing Temple project and this is Vincent Pargeter, the county millwright. Did you know that Essex is the only county with its own millwright?'

'What are you up to?'

'They're dismantling the chaff-cutter. I've donated it to Crossing Temple.'

Up in Crossing, on a farm formerly belonging to Mr Cullen, where the local pony club had used to hold its annual gymkhanas, was the site of Crossing Temple, the great house built by the knights of St John in the twelfth century. The house itself had long since been dismantled or destroyed, but the three massive barns, which had been used to store the corn, still remained, the oldest and largest barns from that period still in use. David Andrews was in charge of co-ordinating the preservation of the historic site and I was pleased that the chaff-cutter had found such a good home.

'Now,' said Roger, as we sat down to lunch of microwaved kippers. 'Do you want to hear about the biological impulses which govern all economic activity?'

'I do, I do,' I replied, 'but first I want to find a napkin. This melting butter is dribbling everywhere.'

I opened the end drawer of the dresser where the napkins and tablecloths used to be kept in my childhood. There they all were. Clearly the drawer hadn't been opened for 30 years. I rummaged through the tablecloths on the top and saw a photograph, sticking up along the side of the drawer from the joint in the corner. I picked it out. It was a photograph of Anne and Juliet standing outside on the step leading into the courtyard. Anne looked about 14, Juliet 12.

Anne was standing stiffly to attention, shoulders back, chin out, staring bravely at the camera through round National Health glasses. She was wearing old-fashioned jodhpurs with baggy thighs which looked much too big for her, so that I wondered if they had been passed down by my mother, and a tweed hacking jacket, which conversely looked much too small. Her dark, wavy hair, another inheritance from our mother, bunched out at either side of her pale face.

Juliet was bending over, looking questioningly at the photographer, as she fondled the head of Liz, our Alsatian bitch, who stood between the two girls. She was wearing jeans and a shapeless sweater and looked uncertain as to whether she should be looking at the camera or attempting to restrain the dog. I imagined that her straight, dark hair had been inherited from our father, but had never been able to test the theory, since he had no hair at all, apart from some grey tufts around his ears and the back of his head, having been completely bald from the age of 20.

I was struck by how the characteristic poses exemplified the personalities of my two sisters. As a girl, Anne had been an organized, determined, get-on-with-it sort of person, so that Juliet called her 'bossy boots'. Juliet was a quieter, softer, more hesitant sort of girl. Her school friends called her Pixie and the nickname suited her.

As girls, neither of them had been able to handle our father's argumentative and opinionated ways. He, for his part, could not understand that his two daughters did not have degrees in Law, with which to counter his statements for the prosecution, or why, whenever they were making a racket or, in Juliet's case, crying with earache, to which she was prone, it would always be at the foot of the stairs, outside the dining-room door, where he would spend most of the weekends, preparing his briefs. I, early on, learned the importance of bolt holes.

Conversation between my father and my sisters was marked by mutual incomprehension which, in their teenage years, turned to a remote formality and, on bad days, to antipathy. My father had the irritating habit of switching from harshly delivered criticism to a kind of gushing sentimentality, largely because he had a guilty conscience that he had been too hard on the girls but, because he overdid both the criticism and the sentimentality, this only made matters worse.

I was more fortunate than Anne and Juliet and never got into the emotional arguments that were so distressing to them. Whether it was because I was a boy, or because I was the youngest and didn't receive the same impatient treatment, or whether it was because I had inherited my mother's temperament, I am not sure. If I was the object of his displeasure and there was no bolt hole handy, I would either argue with a stubborn and unreasoning intractability, or else I just walked away. Intransigence and absence were two weapons that he could not handle. I discovered a third, when I was a strapping 15 and he spent one entire Sunday lunchtime criticizing my dress, my speech, my table manners and my school report.

Being unable to respond to the criticism, probably because it was true, but resenting the sarcastic tone of voice, I threatened to thump him. My sisters and my mother gasped in shocked disbelief at this open rebellion in the genteel surroundings of the dining-room. My father blustered on for a few seconds and then fell silent and I had learned that he may have been a successful barrister, but he didn't fancy a loose ruck with the Under XVIs' open side, wing forward.

My sisters, however, did not have the same remedies in their hands, either temperamental or physical. Anne, who had a similar combative temperament to my father, would stand her ground gamely and attempt to respond logically. Being less experienced and having no ultimate deterrent in her arsenal, she invariably lost and would stalk off, clenching her fists and muttering with indignation. Juliet, with her softer nature, never hearing the words, but registering the tone of voice, would burst into tears and slink away with hurt feelings, wondering how anyone could be so horrid.

Both girls would seek refuge with my mother on these occasions and there would be awkward and atmosphere-laden whisperings in the scullery, which always seemed to me to be more damaging to the whisperers than the whispered about. They resolved nothing and perpetuated the antipathy, when a good row might have cleared the air.

Later, when the girls left home and started work in London, their visits home were marked by a remote stiffness and later still, when they had both married and emigrated, the remoteness became emphasized by distance. I was sorry that neither of them had had an effective weapon with which to counter their father on the battlefield of family life and I was sorry that they had seldom had the opportunity to see him away from Fulford Mill, or to spend much time with him later in his life, when the pressure of work had abated and he didn't spend all weekend on his cases.

He retired as a practising barrister at the age of 55 and became a county court judge, sitting at Bloomsbury and Marylebone County Court. He stayed at his flat in the Inner Temple during the week and being of a gregarious nature, he joined two London clubs, Boodles and the Athenaeum. Since at that time I was working in central London, he would quite often invite me to have dinner with him and we spent many pleasant evenings in the elegant first-floor dining-room at Boodles and sitting in the comfortable, leather armchairs in the downstairs lounge, sipping port and talking about nothing in general and everything in particular.

I came to know him not as a father, but as an individual and found he was a caring and affectionate person beneath his intimidating exterior, with a surprising sense of humour. To my further surprise, he was acutely aware of his own shortcomings, regretting that he had been unable to reach a closer relationship with my sisters and acknowledging his own part in that failure.

'You know how it is,' he said one evening, when he was in a reflective mood. 'You get caught up in your work. You've done it yourself, working long hours and bringing work home. Then, when you can ease up a bit, you find your children have grown up and left home and you wonder what it was all about.'

'You were very hard on the girls.'

'I was, wasn't I. It was only because I was so bound up with my work. I thought that was my role. I regret it now.'

He was in his early seventies at this time and his immobility was getting worse, so that he walked with a slow shuffle. As we left the club, I helped him on with his overcoat and walked slowly with him to the top of St James's. My car was parked in the garage of my office, nearby in Arlington Street.

'Are you sure I can't give you a lift back to the Temple?' I asked.

'No, I think I'll just walk down Piccadilly a little way and get the bus. It drops me at the top of Middle Temple Lane. I'd like a little walk.'

I left him and walked across St James's to Bennet Street. I turned at the corner and watched, as he slowly shuffled round the corner of Piccadilly, dabbing his eyes with a white handkerchief. I wished my sisters could have witnessed the moment of vulnerability and I wished, too, that he hadn't found it so hard, but love is never simple.

My own relationship with my sisters was easy-going and unpressured. There was never any tension and we offered each other the same courtesies that you would extend to a stranger, for that is what we were. Being younger than they, by the time I went to St Margaret's they were higher up the school and our paths seldom crossed. By the time I went to Summer Fields, they had moved on to New Hall and our lives became even more separate. We would live under the same roof at Fulford Mill during the holidays, but they did not want a younger brother tagging along in their more grown-up games and by that time I had discovered football and cycling and friends of my own.

When they had left school and were working in London, I would only see them on their irregular weekend visits to Fulford Mill and, even then, we would each be involved with our own activities. After they had emigrated and all three of us had married, our paths naturally crossed even less and since I was an unreliable correspondent, months and even years would pass without communication. It didn't seem to matter much. We had never been integral to each other's lives. We had all gone our different ways and on the occasions when we did meet, or spoke on the telephone at Christmas or on birthdays, there was an easy rapport. We seemed each to have an instinctive understanding of what we could and couldn't say, how we each felt and how we would react to any given set of circumstances.

I had felt some trepidation after my father's death, when it came to dividing up our parents' valuables. Having seen the bickering over my Great Uncle Walter's will, I was concerned that the division of our parents' possessions should not be the cause of a family feud.

Both our parents had inherited and acquired some nice pieces of antique furniture, silver, china and objets d'art and naturally there were pieces that more than one of us would have liked. However, when the time came to make a list of who should have what, negotiations were conducted with a holding back and deference to the wishes of each other, to such an extent that I wondered at one stage if I would ever get the house cleared.

Transatlantic telephone calls with Juliet:

'Would you like the oak gate-leg table?'

'Well, I've got a spot for it, but Anne likes it.'

'What about the Georgian candlesticks?'

'They'd go really well in your dining-room. What about Ma's bureau?'

'Would you like that? What about Granny's, they're almost identical, although Granny's needs repairing.'

'Anne doesn't want one, she's got one of her own. I'll swap you the bedside commodes and the teak garden furniture for Ma's bureau.'

'No, no. If you want, you can have it. I'll have Granny's.'

'No, you have it. I like the patio furniture.'

'I'll have Granny's mended and we can decide later.'

Anne from Dublin:

'What Juliet really wants is the dining-table and chairs, but she doesn't want to say so.'

'Well, I don't want them, do you? I'd wish she'd say.'

'I'm going to send you back the silver inkstand that used to stand on Pa's desk. You haven't got enough bits and pieces like that.'

'I thought I'd send the antique glasses that Ma collected over to Juliet.'

'Who's going to have the grandfather clock? It is too tall for my house and Juliet's.'

'I could probably find a home for it, but it needs mending. It doesn't work.'

Most of the furniture and objects were suffering from some degree of Millitis, but fortunately, both Coggeshall, near Fulford Mill and Dorking, near my home in Surrey, were centres for antique dealers and had their own cottage industry of repairers and restorers. I became an expert in French polishing, the application of mahogany veneer, horology, enamel inlay, the treatment of frogging and other more arcane areas of the restorer's craft, known only to Lovejoy, as I had damaged items repaired.

At Sotheby's, Christie's and Phillip's I learned about Chinese jade, medals and memorabilia, Brazilian and Sri Lankan emeralds, the carats, colour and facets of South African diamonds and the appraisal of sterling silver from the hallmarks of its assay office and date letter, as we divided up my mother's jewellery and the collection of silver.

The restorers of Coggeshall and Dorking bought timeshares in the Algarve from the proceeds of my visits and Witham International Removals moved to a modern building in Chelmsford, as shipments criss-crossed the Atlantic and the Irish sea, until finally each of us was left with a collection of items that weren't our first choice, but which we felt we ought to have, because neither of the others seemed to want them.

The kippers were finished, there was butter on my napkinless knees. Roger placed his hands flat on the kitchen table, in a gesture of a school teacher demanding attention. 'So that is my argument. Now tell me, what have you learned?'

I had been vaguely aware of his voice in the background, as I drifted through my own reverie, but I hadn't heard a word of what he had said. It had been the same at university when some highly qualified professor had been attempting to instil into me the principles of macro-economics, while I was contemplating the fingerwork of Blues guitar.

'I've learned why I had a struggle to pass my degree and you passed yours with flying colours.'

By 8.30 next morning Charlie was at work with the cement-mixer in the courtyard, mixing concrete to line the floor of the small, sentry-box-sized shed by the front wall, where the mains water stopcock had been placed and where the spring water pipe ended in a tap to be convenient for watering the garden during any future hosepipe bans. Presumably flowers are indifferent to dead rat.

I felt dissatisfied. It had not been a good week for me. I had wasted many hours with my car and felt that I had not achieved much. The car wouldn't start properly again this morning, despite the six new injectors. I rang my local garage in Surrey and booked it in for Monday, thinking I would have to use my mother's mini to drive down to Fulford next week. It had stood in the first garage, unused and neglected from the time of my mother's death in 1986, until I had replaced the corroded battery and it had started first time.

After breakfast, in order to feel that I had achieved something during the week, I began to clear out the cellar, starting by dismantling the rotten, wooden storage racks and passing them out through the side grill into the lane from where I could carry them up to the stable yard and add them to the bonfire site there.

The door at the top of the cellar stairs closed and I heard the bolt being drawn. I took no notice. Roger was fooling around. I went on dismantling. I heard the bolt being withdrawn and the door opened, then it closed again and once again the heavy sound of the bolt being drawn. Curious, I went to the foot of the stairs and looked up.

'What's happening?' I called up the stairs.

Roger's face appeared at the door.

'Oh, I was just practising being a Bearman,' he grinned.

'And what have you discovered?'

'Mmm, highly compulsive behaviour. I wonder if he had an inferiority complex.'

'I think he just wanted to make sure he had turned the light off.'

'Yes, yes, but he could have done that by making a point of turning it off when he got to the top of the stairs.'

Thinking of the countless times that I had gone purposefully into a room and having got there, thought 'What did I come here for?' and having put my middle-aged forgetfulness down to the rapid erosion of the brain cells, I defended the then middle-aged Bearman. 'Well he was always a conscientious man.'

Lunch was Double Delights. Roger's was real chicken with coleslaw, mine was Cumberland sausage in bacon and egg mayonnaise. Roger made a cup of tea for me and a boiling water with skimmed milk for himself. We opened our cellophane packages and I took out my Delight. It had the weight and consistency of drying cement. His theme for the day was the history of the bathing arrangements at Fulford Mill.

'Of course, in the seventeen hundreds, there wouldn't have been any bathrooms as we know them today. For bathing the members of the family would have had hip-baths, which would be brought to the bedroom and filled with hot water by the servants, but that wouldn't have happened more than once a week. For everyday washing, each bedroom would have a washstand.'

I took a bite of my DD and wondered briefly if I had the telephone number of my dentist.

'What about toilet arrangements?'

It was a foolish question.

'Well, before Thomas Crapper revolutionized toilets there would have been commodes in each of the bedrooms and one downstairs, where the toilet is now.'

I wondered what kind of septic tank would have existed at Fulford Mill before Charlie Binder had carried out his own twentieth-century revolution to the Victorian cesspit by the tail water, thinking how appropriate the names of these master craftsmen were. Fortunately, I was unable to make further inquiries along these lines, as Roger had progressed to an exposition on the architectural design of the communal toilets of the Romans. My appetite seemed to have gone. I opened the biscuit jar and resorted to the safety of a McVitie's digestive.

Chapter Seven

I left my car with the local garage on Monday morning and took the train to London to catch up on some neglected business matters. When I returned, Gary greeted me on the garage forecourt.

'It's running fine now. I've just retuned it. Sometimes these transplants don't take first time.'

I drove down to the Mill next morning, arriving at 11 o'clock. Robert Ridgewell was in the forecourt with Terry and Melvin, laying out the concrete kerb which would form the boundary of the gravelled area. I put my case on the doorstep of the lane door, while I looked over the fence at what they were doing. Roger came round the fence from the garden.

'Ah, Charles, I've taken an executive decision in your absence.'

He led me by the arm to the septic tank with its retaining wall.

'I've asked George to give the decking another coat of creosote, because it's drying out fast. Also, I've asked Robert to leave a nine-inch gap between the kerb and the wall of the tank. I thought you'd want to soften the line with some planting. Vinca would be nice.'

'It seems sensible to me,' I replied, wondering if I could dispense with the journeys from Surrey and make do with a weekly progress report in the form of 'executive decisions' from Roger and just send regular infusions of cash. I carried on into the house by the kitchen door and put the kettle on. Roger came in by the lane door, bearing my case and waving my key.

'This man is a security risk. He's only been here two minutes and already he's left his key in the door.'

'That way I know where it is.'

It transpired that our theme for the day was women's dress. 'Until Beau Brummel invested the trouser early in the last century, men also wore a kind of dress or skirt arrangement. Of course there were doubloons and knee breeches and tights for military or theatrical purposes, but the everyday man's wear was the smock. After Brummel, men took to wearing trousers because of their practicality and women were left with the dress. That was true up until the advent of the Pill. Then women were able to become an economic unit themselves and started to graduate to trousers.'

I thought back as he spoke and reflected that I couldn't remember ever having seen my mother in trousers and the only time I saw my sisters in them as girls was when they were riding. My girlfriends always seemed to be wearing skirts or dresses in my memory.

'It's all part of the marginalization of men,' Roger continued. 'Once women were able to become economically free and the Pill made pregnancy an option, rather than a certainty, women began to see men as a choice, rather than a necessity. Since women are biologically the nurturers and food providers and men are the providers only of territory, or income, then they began to be marginalized by women and we have moved towards a matriarchal society rather than a patriarchal one.'

'So eventually we will be completely redundant.'

'Theoretically yes, except as a status symbol or servant or a househusband in the family role. We would still have our individual roles in our work or profession, but it won't necessarily be linked to marriage or supporting a family. You see this happening now. Women are choosing to marry later, or not get married at all, even when they have children, and not to stay in unsatisfactory marriages. Men are choosing to marry later or not get married at all, since there are so many available women. They can have the enjoyment without the responsibility.'

'Hmm,' I mused. I thought it was unlikely that I had much future as a status symbol and the servant role didn't sound very appetizing, but househusband! Now that sounded promising.

'This househusband role, Roger. Could I stay at home and kiss my wife goodbye as she set off for work?'

'A good many men do that now.'

'I could have househusband's coffee mornings, or perhaps even better Scotch mornings.'

'You seem to be entering into the spirit of it.'

'Well, it seems to have certain advantages.'

I contemplated the conversation at my Scotch mornings.

'Did you know that Henry's wife has been made regional manager?'

'I suppose they'll move into a bigger house.'

'Henry will enjoy doing up a new house. This is very good scotch, Charles.'

'Yes, it's a ten-year-old malt I got from that off-licence behind Bank Street, where Michael bought the Australian Chardonnay when he had his wine and cheese. Weren't the canapés good and he made them all himself.'

'He probably bought them from Marks and hid the wrappers.'

I was clearly hallucinating. Was it the influence of Fulford Mill or Roger Tabor?

Thursday. Seven-thirty and Colin Ridgewell's JCB was delivered by lorry. I came downstairs to find the forecourt awash with metal. Apart from the massive digger itself, there was an assortment of alternative tools, blades ranging in length from three feet to five feet and a collection of different-shaped steel buckets.

At nine o'clock the high pressure water jet, which I had rented for the day from HSS Hire, was delivered. I thought that it might be effective in removing the accumulated coal dust from the face of the bricks lining the cellar floor. I spent the morning trying to assemble it. By twelve o'clock it was complete. Flushed with my success, I turned my attention to the date inset on my watch.

After lunch, Colin arrived to check that the machinery had been delivered so that his team could start grading the forecourt next day. He stood on the step of the lane door, next to the dining-room window, looking up at the fifth floor overhang of the Mill, which contained a trapdoor for hauling sacks of corn to the top of the Mill without the need for going inside.

'Hello, Charles,' he said, as I answered his ring at the door. 'I was just looking up at that old trapdoor. I remember during the war we had an army exercise here. Army versus the Home Guard it was. Mr Blyth, or Captain Blyth, I should say, was the officer commanding the Home Guard and we were the other ranks. Everyone here at the Mill was exempt from National Service because we were doing an essential trade, but the Army used to come round every now and again to keep us on our toes. Anyway, I was standing here, where I am now, when an Army bren-gun carrier came round the Mill corner. Well, we didn't have any weapons to defend ourselves, so young Arthur Sutton opened that trapdoor and threw a brick down on the bren-gun carrier. It bounced off the armour-plated shield and went straight through the dining-room window there. Captain Blyth wasn't at all happy.

' "Huh," he said, "the only damage I've had in this entire war is from one of my own men." '

Roger had come out of the Mill and joined us, as Colin recounted the story.

'You must know the Mill well?' he said.

'Well, I know it well, but I've never been up above the ground floor,' Colin replied.

'Would you like to come up now?'

'Yes, I'd be very interested.'

'I'll just get my tape-recorder and I'll tape our conversation. I'm sure you've got a lot of interesting tales to tell.'

They went off into the Mill and I descended to the cellar and spent a watery afternoon, jetting and scrubbing at the coal dust. It made no discernible difference. It was a cold day and the chill permeated the cellar. By five o'clock I was cold and wet and could no longer see what I was doing by the light of the single, 40-watt bulb at the bottom of the stairs. I went back upstairs, had a quick wash, and sat in the dining-room, reviewing the programme to date.

Ten minutes later, Roger came in from the dark and cold Mill, wearing a calf-length, brown overcoat of indescribable decrepitude and great age. It looked to me as if it had experienced an excess of fulling.

'I'll have you know,' he pronounced importantly at my startled expression, 'that this overcoat was around in the First World War.'

'It probably caused it.'

'Huh! You're a fine one to talk. When did you last shave?'

'It's designer stubble. If I walked down Banktree High Street now, young girls would mob me thinking I was George Michael.'

'You'd be thrown in the slammer as a vagrant.'

Friday morning and the deep-throated engine of the JCB greeted my breakfast. It was a wonderful, winter morning with a crispness in the air and the sun glinting through the oak by the cottage. After breakfast I went into the living-room, where Roger was replaying the tape of his conversation with Colin in the Mill. He was overjoyed with the result.

'This is wonderful, Charles. This is a man who used to bring corn to the Mill in a tumbril and leave it on the ground floor and then collect it again, after it had been milled. Dick Weller would drop the sacks into the tumbril from the platform.'

'Yes, he must remember the Mill from his youth.'

'He tells me that "every square foot about these parts tells a tale". He'd never been upstairs in the Mill before and he was most interested in the workings. When we got upstairs he started telling quite a few stories of his time here. Listen to this.'

We listened to Colin's soft, deep, careful voice recounting how the sacks would be tied by chain and drawn up through the sequence of heavy, double leafed trapdoors.

'It's wonderful, isn't it?' Roger enthused, 'he's got such a perfect radio voice. It reminds me of that Hampshire cricket commentator.'

He was getting carried away.

'Yes,' I replied, 'have you heard his programme *Essex Tales* on Radio Four?'

'What?'

'Perhaps he'd give you a tape if you asked.'

'Quite, quite.'

I wandered over to the window and watched the digger being manipulated on the forecourt. It was mesmerizing. Brian, its driver, was a stocky man in his thirties with dark, curly hair. His face was impassive as he sat in the enclosed cab with windows on all four sides. He had the big, pronged bucket on one hydraulic arm of the digger and a four-foot blade on the other.

The area of the forecourt was 50 feet long and 40 feet deep. It was bounded on the lane side by the hedge, on the house side by a flower border of hollyhocks, feverfew and irises, on the garden side by the sweep of the new, concrete kerbing and on the river side by the retaining wall of the septic tank. Within this area, there were the further obstacles of the two manhole covers which contained the junction point for the drain runs and the inspection chamber for the electric cabling for the tank.

The huge, yellow digger was 30 feet long with its arms extended and weighed six and a half tons. There seemed to be no spare space within the confined area in which it could move in order to spread the massive pile of crushed concrete which had been deposited by the septic tank and still miss the manhole covers.

Brian sat at the controls. The only part of him that moved was his arms. The buckets rose, the digger set down two of its foot square, metal feet and it twisted to the right. Brian pushed another lever and the other two feet fell, as the first two rose. The huge machine waddled forward, missing the circular manhole containing the electric cables by two inches. The big bucket swung down, scooping up half a ton of crushed concrete, missing the wooden decking by an inch. A round pebble fell off the top of the load, rolled over the decking, down the steep bank and plopped into the river. Brian's face registered annoyance. He pushed one lever and pulled another. The huge bucket adjusted its hold on the heavy load of concrete, as if it were shaking rubbish down into a plastic bin-liner to make it more compact. Satisfied, he backed the machine past the first manhole cover, missing it by four inches, swivelled the digger, missing the second manhole cover by an inch, backed, missing the narrow, concrete kerbing by three inches, lowered the bucket and shook out the load at the foot of Robert's spade, as he stood, pointing out the target area. A spadeful landed on the second manhole cover.

'Don't worry, Brian, I'll move that,' Robert shouted, but he was too late. Already the huge bucket had been lowered and drawn back, brushing the offending rubble off the fragile surface of the manhole with the lightness of a feather duster. The margin of error could only have been a millimetre. I was watching a master at work. Roger joined me at the window.

'Have you got any classical music, Rog?'

'Yes, what do you want.'

'Well, either something gentle like a Bach piano concerto, or something vigorous, a Klemperer orchestration.'

'What do you want it for?' he asked as he put a Bach piece on his record player.

'This would make a wonderful film,' I replied, as he rejoined me at the window. The resonant notes filled the room as the huge, metal ballet dancer turned, pirouetted and twisted to the music on the forecourt, its own throaty engine drowned by the soaring violins.

By 10.30, eight tons of crushed concrete had been laid and levelled. The hoggin was due to arrive by 11, but it was late. Robert and Terry laid a small, brick, edging wall in front of the hedge. I went outside to watch their careful work. Terry looked up at me, as I stood at the top of the flight of five wide stone steps leading up to the front door.

'It would look better if we replaced these flettons along the border, with the old red bricks we're using for the rest of the border.'

I nodded. 'Yes it would.'

They were all like that, always looking for work and always trying to improve the result.

By 11.30 the hoggin still hadn't arrived. Brian was becoming impatient. He climbed down from his cab and went to help Robert and Terry as they back-filled the trench of the retaining wall for the tank.

At 11.45 the first load of hoggin arrived. The lorry tipped a small mountain of the reddish, orange clay mixed with aggregate at the entrance by the gate. There was a rush of activity. Brian climbed back into his cab and positioned the JCB by the pile. Robert, Terry and Melvin each took one of the three builder's wheelbarrows and lined up by the pile, while Colin collected a wide, wooden rake from his pickup and stood by the flower bed under the living-room window, which was to form the limit of the forecourt. Brian picked up a scoop of hoggin in the smaller bucket and dumped it into Robert's wheelbarrow. There was far too much. The barrow was filled to overflowing and the surplus spilled on the ground. Robert wheeled the barrow at the run to his father while Brian scooped up the fallen surplus, picked up a half-load and dumped it in Terry's barrow. Terry ran across the uneven surface of crushed concrete and dropped it at Colin's feet. Robert was already back in the queue behind Melvin as Brian dropped the next scoop into his wheelbarrow and he ran in Terry's path to where Colin was calmly raking out the heavy, orange clay into a perfect gradient.

I went upstairs to the landing at the front of the house and looked down through the wide Georgian window, as the digger deposited its heavy loads with perfect rhythm and the three young men ran with the unwieldy barrows, over the treacherous surface of the rubble, to where the older man methodically translated their youthful energy into a smooth, even surface. I had never seen a team game played with such perfect understanding. In 20 minutes they had laid and raked ten tons of hoggin. It seemed like the birth of a new era as the old eighteenth-century carriageway was transformed into a forecourt for the carriages of the twentieth century.

I went downstairs and once again stood at the top of the stone steps. Moving in and out between the works being carried out in the forecourt and the relatively unchanged house from the memories of my childhood, with its hall wallpaper now 70 years old, the blue-painted, panelled front door came to symbolize in my mind that fleeting nano-second which we call the present.

It was as if the house, with its weight of history, was the past and the energy, enthusiasm and change being expressed by Robert, Terry and Melvin in the forecourt represented the future. Passing through the front door, from one to the other, was a frozen moment in time, like the click of the shutter on my Nikon and I felt unnerved by its insignificance in the endless roll of eternity.

Talfryn, who likes to write poetry in his spare time, of which he has such an abundant supply that he could have written an epic of *Paradise Lost* proportions, had, by a bizarre coincidence, penned some lines on the same subject:

'Said the Future to the Past, a thought has crossed my mind.
You grow ever larger as destiny unwinds.
Do you ever think, as you grow so big and tall,
One day you'll be so gross, that on the Present you will fall?
The Past heaved a sigh as he reclined on the chaise-longue,
'Why is it,' he said tersely, 'that you always get things
     wrong?
The Present is a moment that is so very small,
That his passing would be noticed by nobody at all.'

Monday, as usual, was spent in my office, attempting to keep the wolf prowling at some distance from the door. I drove down in the evening and arrived at Fulford Mill late.

I had a bad night. I woke up with a start at 4.15 from a curious dream in which I had stolen a London bus. I was driving it along Leytonstone High Road and had stopped to pick up some passengers, when another bus approached from the opposite direction. Recognizing the number of my bus, the driver called out 'Morning, Reg,' as he drew level, then seeing my unfamiliar face, he slammed on his brakes, thrusting the faces of the passengers into their morning newspapers. Realizing that the game was up, I leapt out of the cab, planning on escaping through an adjoining council estate. I landed in an untidy mess on the road and woke up on the floor with a splitting headache.

I was unable to get back to sleep, as I lay attempting to analyse this incomprehensible dream and finally, at 6.30 I got up, vowing to steer clear of Roger's Bulgarian vodka in future. He had offered me a glass on my late arrival the previous evening.

'This is chimney sweep's vodka,' he said solemnly.

'What do you mean?'

'One glass of this will sweep your chimney.'

He demonstrated by throwing an eighth of a glass on to the open fire. There was a resounding 'woompf' and a fireball, reminiscent of scenes from *Apocalypse Now*, burst up the chimney, causing a drizzle of black soot to cascade over the burning logs.

I went down to the kitchen and made a cup of coffee and sat in my blue, striped nightshirt and Marks & Spencer socks, looking out of the window. On Friday, Charlie had been banned from the forecourt, where he had been erecting the new fence, while Colin and his team laid the concrete and hoggin. Grumpily, he had spent the day lowering the level of the courtyard wall in an orange and black Rastafarian bonnet. Now I had an unhindered view into the garden. There had been a frost during the night and the garden was covered in a fine layer of white. The pale yellow faces of the primroses peeped shyly from the border which lined the grey stone path to the terrace and the short, emerald shoots of the wakening daffodils stood in silent clusters in the opaque light. On the tennis court, two early blackbirds hopped purposefully in search of their due reward. There was no breeze and a light mist hung motionless in the still air, shrouding the valley in silence.

By 7.30, a pale winter sun began to melt through the mist and the garden sparkled as the weak rays reflected like crystal from the terrace. My headache evaporated with the frost.

It started again at eight o'clock, as the ear-splitting chatter of a pneumatic drill exploded in the forecourt. I looked out of the dining-room window. Robert was attacking the rock-hard concrete containing the kerb stones of the lane where the new access was to be formed. I took two Nurofen and got dressed.

Charlie and George arrived to continue work on the new fence while I drove into Banktree and picked up the Supa-Stork wheel grinder which I had hired to continue with my efforts to remove the compacted coal dust in the cellar. It had failed to respond to the high-pressure water jet and clearly something more serious was needed. Returning to the house, I found that Janka, Roger's voluptuous, twenty-year-old Croatian cleaning lady was busy with the hoover. In my experience, cleaning ladies were always middle-aged, grey-haired and called Mrs A. Obviously Roger cast his domestic help with the same care that he employed in his films.

We had a brief skirmish as to whether the extension cable was better employed creating dust, attached to my Supa-Stork, or sucking it up, attached to her vacuum-cleaner. I lost and, fearing for the Serbs, picked up the post as a consolation prize. To my surprise there was a letter for me. A business colleague had managed to track me down at Fulford Mill. This was no mean feat, as Annette normally disclaims all knowledge of my whereabouts to those unfortunates from the business world who ring my home in the hope of locating me; a habit which has led to an interesting reduction in my commercial activities and ensures that I am unlikely to suffer from stress.

I read the letter and realized that for a while I was going to have to don my business suit, if only figuratively, and concentrate on the valuation of some commercial property assets on behalf of a company which retained me as a consultant.

I went into the dining-room and sat at the paper-strewn table, trying to imagine that it was my fully equipped work station at home, to put me in the frame of mind for the task in hand. It didn't work. Somehow, my dirty jeans, torn sweater and unshaven face were not conducive to assessing the value of a rent review on a warehouse in Coulsdon. I realized that I was suffering from a hitherto unrecorded form of Millitis, involving total divorce from the real world.

By four o'clock, the future of Coulsdon was assured and the Croatian Amazon had withdrawn to her bunker. Unopposed, I commandeered the extension cable and lugged the heavy Supa-

Stork down into the cellar. It worked a treat. The floor was still damp from my jetting and the scouring motion of the cylindrical head lifted the coal dust from the bricks, revealing their original rust colour. After half an hour, I switched the machine off and stood at the far end of the cellar to survey the effect when the 40-watt bulb expired with an apologetic cough and I was plunged into darkness. As I stepped carefully through the coiled cable of the Supa-Stork, I heard the cellar door being closed and the bolt being drawn. Roger was fooling around again. I climbed the stairs in the dark and called through the door.

'Come on, Rog. The light bulb's gone.'

To my horror I heard the lane door slam shut. As quickly as I could in the pitch black, I scuttled down the stairs and ran to the iron grill of the coal chute, just in time to see the tail lights of his Polo disappearing up the lane towards Crossing.

'Roger!'

My voice echoed forlornly through the hollow cellar. I stood, staring intently up the lane, willing the film to run backwards, for the tail lights of the Polo to reappear, for Roger to stride backwards across the lane, open the lane door, scurry backwards down the passage, draw the bolt of the cellar door and release me from my damp, cold and dark dungeon. It had no effect. I was a prisoner of Fulford Mill.

I sat down on the brick plinth among the imaginary casks of ale. There was no way I could get out on my own, that much was certain. I was alone in the house, the window at the garden end had been filled in and the window at the lane end was blocked by iron bars thicker than those at Wormwood Scrubs.

How long would he be gone? Had he just gone up to the station to collect Liz and would be back in ten minutes, or had he gone to Chelmsford to give his adult education lecture and wouldn't be back until ten, or had he had enough of the English climate and the conversion of the Mill, packed his bags and emigrated to the Seychelles, never to return?

Paranoia set in with the night. The last glimmers of dusk faded from the western sky over the mill pool and the outline of the building melted into the inky black, as I stood looking up through the grill of my prison.

By eight o'clock he still had not returned. I had left my anorak upstairs and the damp chill of the night seeped through my thin sweater. I paced the cellar in the darkness to keep my circulation moving and attempted to recite 'Ode to a Nightingale' to keep my brain ticking over. I couldn't remember it. Was I dying from exposure or just middle-aged? I began to sneeze, as I heard the familiar rattle of the nine o'clock train to Albaton. It registered dully in my brain. Of course! Sometimes the hospital workers returned from Witham on the train and walked down the lane back to their digs in Black Nutleam. I scurried back to the grill, listening intently for the sound of a pedestrian and heard the scuffle of a single pair of shoes echoing against the Granary.

'Hello! Hello!' I called from my subterranean cell.

The feet stopped and a startled, oriental voice cried in the blackness: 'Who's that?'

'Down here. I'm down here,' I called.

The feet turned round quickly on the spot. The pedestrian bent over, peering into my pitch-black recess and I saw the staring whites of a pair of terrified eastern eyes. 'Aiee,' he exclaimed, scuttling sideways across the lane into the lee of the Mill.

'Come back, come back,' I cried, but his feet were running round the Mill corner and disappearing up the rise to Black Nutleam, with the speed of Linford Christie.

Fearing the haemorrhoids of the brick plinth, I sat on the top step of the stairs, huddled against the corner of the door, composing my will, when the sound of the heavy latch of the lane door being opened shattered my attempt to remember the postal address of Amnesty International.

'Roger! Roger!'

The bolt of the cellar door was drawn back and a triangle of light blinded my dark-accustomed eyes.

'Goodness, you're working late. What are you doing there in the dark?'

'I'm just establishing why Bearman used to check the door.'

Wednesday I spent in bed nursing my cold and a huff.

Thursday I went downstairs for breakfast and found that Roger had left a large, printed message in front of my chair on a piece of A4 paper: 'Keep the cats in today.'

This was the day that the bitumen emulsion was to be sprayed over the hoggin to hold it in position before the gravel was spread and he was anxious that Leroy should not go outside and walk on it, with his insatiable curiosity and either get stuck, or spend hours licking the liquid asphalt from his paws, doing irreparable damage to his digestive system.

I checked the cats, as I made toast. They were sitting nonchalantly in the scullery next to the three boxes of cat litter, which Roger had thoughtfully prepared the day before in readiness for their day of imprisonment. Not satisfied with the quantity of cat litter which he had left, he had instructed me to buy another bag from a specific pet shop on the Coggeshall Road.

'What sort do you want?'

'I can't remember the name, but it's grey. They won't have anything to do with it if it's white or has blue granules in it.'

I arrived at the shop he had specified and it was shut. Wondering what to do, I went to Tesco's to complete my shopping and discovered that they sold cat litter. I stood in front of the pet care section, considering the four different varieties which lined the shelf. Which one was grey? There was no way of knowing short of breaking open the sealed bags. I stopped a passing housewife with some tins of Whiskas in her trolley.

'Excuse me, do you know which of these is grey?'

'Put 'em out in the garden luv.'

With this robust advice, I approached a teenager in a red Tesco coat with matching acne.

'Are you an expert on cat litter?'

'No, I'm an expert on dried foods. You want the supervisor. It's his day off.'

'I selected a bag at random, praying for it to be grey and returned to the house. Roger opened it apprehensively.

'Is it grey?' I asked.

'Not exactly. It's more red with green granules.'

'Well, they're not blue granules anyway.'

'Some of them are blue. Oh well, we'll try it anyway.'

He poured some into a plastic tray and set it next to the tray containing the sparse covering of grey litter and stood, looking at them thoughtfully.

'I think I'll do another tray with some plain earth.'

He went out into the garden and dug up some earth and placed it in a third tray next to the other two. His research into toilet traditions and his experience of cats were being employed to the full and I bowed to his superior knowledge.

'They must like one of them,' I ventured encouragingly, concerned that I had failed in my purchasing duties. He hadn't replied.

I ate my Weetabix and Leroy miaowed at me, rubbing his body against my leg, a clear indication that it was his breakfast too. I knew from experience that he didn't like Weetabix, so I gave him the remains of yesterday's tin of KiteKat and he sat eating it contentedly as I ate my toast. As I cleared the breakfast plates away, he stood briefly, considering the three alternative toilets and then hopped into my red granules with green spots, dug frantically with his front paws and squatted, with a look of deep concentration on his face.

Vindicated, I put on my boots and anorak to go outside and confer with Robert about grading the surplus top soil down on to the riverbank, before the emulsion arrived. As I went out, I picked up Roger's message and wrote in large capitals at the bottom, 'What cats?'

I left Robert and Terry spraying the gooey emulsion and drove into Banktree to pick up the replacement wheels for the Supa-Stork and a bag of grey cat litter. Roger was delighted, George less so, as I sent him down into the cellar with the Supa-Stork. It turned into another beautiful day as the sun broke through. Robert and Terry finished spraying the emulsion and began barrowing the ten-millimetre shingle from Roger's hard standing, where it had been dumped, to the forecourt. Once again they were running. The sound of George's Supa-Stork echoed up through the cellar door, which he had insisted should be propped open.

I put on my work gloves and went outside for another bonfire in the stable yard and wandered slowly through the garden in the sun. There was a feeling of early spring in the crisp, still air. The twelve-foot Queen Elizabeth rose bush outside the court-yard door, which I had pruned in January to a mere five foot, praying that it would survive my drastic amputation, sported a gratifying canopy of green and dark-red shoots. The japonica, bordering the wall which Charlie had lowered, which I had sim-ilarly pruned, had clusters of vivid, red flowers bursting from its lower shoots. In the long border leading to the terrace, pale pink primroses had flowered to join their yellow brothers. Every one of the 16 rose bushes which George had transplanted from the forecourt was in bud. The four rows of raspberries and the three gooseberry bushes that he had moved from the top of the gar-den, which now formed part of the paddock, had rewarded his care and patience and were budding next to the Blenheim Orange and Red Ellison apple trees, which I had planted 30 years before.

I started my bonfire and was called down to the forecourt by Robert. He and Terry had nearly finished laying the gravel and wanted any last-minute instructions I might have, before clear-ing up their equipment. We walked around the forecourt as Colin arrived to check the finished job. I could find no fault with it, only little improvements here and there, where they had exceeded their brief to do a better job. It was perfect and the gravel surface stretching from the forecourt up the path to the stable yard and down into the shrubbery seemed to tie the whole garden together, givinq it a coherence and meaning that it had never had in my memory.

The four men stood on the smart, new gravel in front of the house while I took a photograph of their smiling faces to send to my sisters.

'Well, Charles, we'd better be off,' said Colin, offering his hand, 'remember me to Anne and Juliet.'

'You've done a wonderful job.' I was sorry to see them go.

'It's been a pleasure for all of us. One last thing, I thought you might like to have this.'

He handed me a tiny, dog-eared photograph of a tawny-maned young man and a dark-haired, ten-year-old boy, clutching two creamy-white ferrets.

'We both had a lot of hair then, Colin.'

'*Sic transit gloria*, Charles.' He smiled. It seems we all spoke Latin then too.

That evening Roger was giving a lecture at the Cramphorn theatre in Chelmsford on 'The Future of Wild Life in East Anglia', I had subtitled it 'Roger Rabbits'.

It was brilliant. He spoke for two and a half hours on the interaction between the growth in human population and the decline in animals species, with particular reference to East Anglia, but spanning the globe, from the impact of population growth in rural India on the survival of the tiger, to the expansion of the Sahel and the subsequent decline of the warbler and the whitethroat. He ranged over the effect of global warming on the weather pattern in sub-arctic Russia and its impact on the number of Brent geese feeding inter-tidally on the Essex coastal marshes. He touched on the disaster of 1976, when a lax Canadian customs official had permitted barked timber to be shipped to Southampton and the careless importation of Dutch Elm disease had led to the destruction of our largest and most numerous, indigenous tree, which in turn had led to the disappearance of the rookery at Fulford Mill and meant that a latter-day Dick Weller had lost one weather portent in deciding whether or not to lower the sluice gate overnight.

He spoke entirely without notes and the audience of 200 sat in rapt and silent attention, carried along by his infectious enthusiasm and encyclopaedic knowledge. As he spoke about the natural habitat surrounding Fulford Mill, which he called 'my mill' and recounted the tales which I had told him, of the otters in the river up until the 1950s, of the Golden Marsh Marigolds and fluffy white Hemp Agrimony, which had lined the banks and of the pink Ragged Robin, growing in profusion in the water meadows, my mind went back to the conversation with David Forrest in November, nearly 18 months before, when we had selected him as the most promising purchaser of the Mill. What an inspired guess it had been.

John Ray, England's foremost naturalist of the seventeenth century, had lived at a house called Dewlands in Black Nutleam on the road into Banktree. His mother had been the local herbalist and it was while tramping the fields surrounding Fulford Mill with her, in her search for medicinal plants, that he had developed his own interest in flora, which had led to the publication of his monumental work, *Historiae Plantarum*. The book is spoken of reverentially by naturalists today and ranks as one of the greatest works of botanical research ever written. I thought how fitting it was, that a twentieth-century naturalist, renowned through the modern medium of television, should be carrying forward his banner of observation and respect for animal and plant species.

Roger had referred to the Mill as 'my mill' before and I had found it strange then. It had worried me, when I had sold it, that I was breaking up an estate which had been held as one for generations and I had confided my doubts to Roger.

'It's strange to hear you call the Mill "my mill". It was always "the" Mill to us. It's often worried me that I am the first person to separate the Mill from the miller's house for 200 years.'

He had reassured me at once with his usual concern, 'You might be the first person for a thousand years.'

He came to the conclusion of his lecture, standing solemnly behind the wooden lectern at the side of the stage. 'Well, folks, the title of this lecture is "The Future of Wild Life in East Anglia". My message to you is simple. Unless we all do something about it now, there isn't going to be one.'

There was a moment's shocked silence and then applause rolled round the large, modern auditorium, reverberating from the Scandinavian pine walls. The audience rose to their feet and swelled down to the front of the stage, chattering and jostling to pay their subscriptions to the Essex Wild Life Trust and I knew that the way to conserve a redundant, eighteenth-century water mill was to entrust it to someone who would call it 'my mill'.

Chapter Eight

The following Wednesday, Ken drove his pickup over to Great Yeldham to collect the outdoor staircase which John Townrow was making for Roger and returned with the new window for the landing, which had been completed earlier than expected. It was six feet tall and three feet wide and needed three of us to carry it up to the landing.

Charlie, in a stylish French beret, collected the sledge-hammer from the top stable and stood on the flat roof of the porch above the lane door, to knock through the opening for the window. He attacked the wall vigorously and an 18-inch square lump of masonry clattered on to the landing. It was a gusty day and the wind picked up the light lime and mortar pointing of the brick-work and shot it through the narrow opening into the house, with the force of a sandblaster. In seconds, I was covered in a film of dust and the red carpet of the hall had turned pink.

'Wait, wait, Charlie!' I cried, 'we'll have to get some dust sheets.'

I ran up to the stable yard and returned with some plastic sheeting. Frantically we tacked the billowing plastic up at the end of the landing, but already the stairs were covered in mortar dust. I left Charlie in his plastic tent and went downstairs. Roger

148

had left two letters addressed to my father on the kitchen table. The top one, in a printed envelope offered 'Quality Services for Deaf People'. In the interests of accuracy, he had crossed out the 'f' and inserted a 'd'. The second, from the Council of Circuit Judges, enclosed a calendar of events for the next law term. Obviously my father's absence from the Inns of Court for the last seven years had not been noticed by the judiciary.

Janka arrived at ten o'clock on her bicycle, in a fluffy pink sweater and tight, black trousers. She directed a withering fusillade of Croatian at me on account of the dust, as I cowered behind a pot of artificial flowers in the hall, unable to find a bolt hole. It was worth it, as she got out a dustpan and brush and began sweeping the stairs, descending backwards as she brushed the treads, giving me a grandstand view of her shapely posterior. It reminded me of Percy and Millicent in Colin's sack.

George came in from the stable yard where he had been creosoting the stable doors. Seeing my ashen face and hearing the muttered, Slavic imprecations issuing from the staircase, he slunk downstairs to continue painting the cellar.

By lunchtime the window opening was complete and the Abominable Snowman in a beret wandered over to the Mill for lunch with Ken and Simon. Roger opened the fridge door.

'Would you like one of these Scotch eggs?'

'No,' I said firmly, having had one before.

'Huh! You Taureans, you're so blunt.'

'What would you like me to be? An indecisive Gemini, I suppose.'

'Yes.'

'All right then. Well, Scotch eggs are a possibility. Perhaps if you put them on the table we can think about them later. You might like one. I wonder if they go with ham?'

'All right, all right. Not so vague.'

'Enthusiastic Sagittarius then. Ah great! Scotch eggs, just what I wanted. What a treat.'

'Now you're going over the top.'

'Argumentative Aquarius? You don't mean Scotch, you mean

Scottish. Actually, of course they originated in Latvia not Scotland.'

Taureans are supposed to be interested in property and it had amused me to discover, when I joined the public property company, which had bought my own company, in 1987, that four of the seven directors had been born under the sign of the bull.

It had often seemed to me that unravelling the influences, which form the behaviour patterns of each of us, is like peeling an onion. The dry, outer husk is the thin veneer imparted by our immediate environment, brittle and easily fractured. The first, inner skin represents the attitudes and values acquired during our upbringing, more resilient and longer-lasting. The thicker, inner layers represent our biology and our instincts, inherited through generations of ancestors and the heart of the vegetable is a core, which even biochemists do not understand, but perhaps astrologers do. Cranky though it may sound in today's practical and scientific world, I had quite often asked the birth sign of someone whose behaviour had seemed to fit into the pattern of a particular sign of the zodiac and, although not being an expert I was often wrong, I was surprised that I was sometimes right. In observing people in this way, I was also struck by the realization that virtues were also vices and vice versa. I discovered that people who were stubborn were also patient, that people who were bigoted were often also principled. It just depended which end of the telescope you were looking through. To my surprise Roger shared my interest in the subject.

'No, I don't think its cranky,' he said. 'Astrology started with the ancient Egyptians and you cannot disregard anything which came from the genius that built the pyramids.'

'But can remote, external influences, like the stars, really affect individual characteristics?'

'Well, let's start with a simpler, more understandable concept. Geophysical considerations certainly affect our physical and physiological makeup. For example, people born in a sunny climate have darker skins and hair than those born in northern countries.'

'Yes, but that's just a result of the sun.'

'Sure, but birth signs are sometimes called Sun signs aren't they? Anyway it doesn't stop there. The people of the Mediterranean have a more relaxed, happy go lucky outlook than the dour Norwegians or the Russians. So a planet, the sun, has influenced their temperament, not just their physical appearance.'

'It's quite a big step from that, to saying that the position of the stars on the day of your birth will determine whether you are creative or narrow-minded, patient or impatient.'

'Not really. The position of the moon determines whether the tide rises or falls at any given time and you are talking about a mass of water on the earth's surface of an incalculable weight. If one planet can exert that monumental influence, it is biochemically conceivable that others can influence the few fluid ounces of chemicals in the human brain.'

'And do you think it is possible to predict the future from an individual horoscope?'

'Definitely.'

'Definitely! That's a strong statement from a Gemini. Give me an example.'

'You're going to cook supper tonight.'

'Ah no, your example fails. It's your turn.'

'Not at all. You're a Taurus. Taureans love their food and I'm going out.'

He grinned and left the table, leaving me to ponder my response.

'I could get a takeaway,' I called.

'Nit-picking,' his voice echoed from the passage.

By the end of the day, the window was in position and fully glazed. The difference was dramatic. As I climbed the stairs, the upper landing was flooded with light, making the corridor to Lucy's bedroom inviting, instead of simulating the gloomy approach to Mrs Danvers's bedroom at Manderley. As an added bonus, there was a delicate and wholly unexpected view, up past the corner of the Mill, through the undulating upper branches of the line of osiers, which bordered the hard standing, to the rise of the pasture meadow beyond. The window had been blocked up in 1856 during the ownership of James Catchpole and I wondered what economic crisis in the milling business had persuaded him that the saving on window tax was more important than the benefits of leaving it in place. Was that the time of the Corn Laws? My history was too rusty. Roger would know.

I spent Thursday morning wandering around the house and grounds with Charlie and George, identifying the remaining jobs. Now that the principle alterations had been completed, there were only minor maintenance problems to attend to. I could have gone on altering and improving the place extensively, but it wouldn't have been cost-effective for my fathers's estate and I didn't want to pre-empt the decisions of the next owner, or dictate their taste. There were bits of tidying up and making good however, which we should finish off. The painting of the cellar and the new window would have to be completed, two of the stable doors needed repair where the ends had rotted over the years and the sill to the bay window needed filling, where it had suffered similar damage. The riverbank beside the septic tank would have to be dug over and receive a copious layer of compost to break up the heavy, chalky boulder clay.

Mick and Nick had been too busy to take on the rewiring of the house, but they had recommended Danbury Electrical Services and their team of electricians were at work neatly and systematically replacing the rubber-cased conduit. I was touched by how carefully they preserved the 70-year-old decor, which would shortly be stripped off by a new owner, but the care and professionalism of the local tradesmen, which was in such stark contrast to their London counterparts, had been one of the unexpected bonuses of undertaking the alterations of the house.

George would have liked to have stayed on, to help me with the gardening, but now that the government had abandoned the ERM and reduced interest rates, the green shoots of recovery were beginning to be seen in the economy, as well as in the garden and he had been approached by the foundry to have his old job back. Charlie stood in the doorway of the first stable, where he was sawing lengths of four by one for the stable doors, as I handed him a mug of tea.

'Not much more to do then, Chas,' he said, pushing a dusty bowler to the back of his head.

'No, that's about the end of it, isn't it?'

'I've got some work in Chelmsford, I could start next week, if you've finished with me.'

'Oh good, I'll give you a ring if I think of anything else.'

'Don't forget me when you do something to that cottage. I'd like to have a go at that.'

I walked back to the house, down the neat, gravel path, where the soggy, clay walls of the mains water trench had been three months before. Apart from the rewiring that was it. The programme which I had set myself six months before was complete. When to start remarketing the house? That was the next question.

The answer arrived next morning, sweeping into the forecourt with a spray of gravel and a black, Springer spaniel.

'This is very posh, Charles!' David Forrest exclaimed, bounding up the front steps, the first visitor to do so for at least 46 years.

I led him upstairs. Fred, the softly spoken and unflappable chief electrician, was busy underneath the new window, dismantling the series of antique, wooden fuse boxes with the care of a brain surgeon. David looked out at the new view.

'This is excellent. What an improvement. Have you finished decorating the new bathroom?'

We went through into the finished bathroom and he sat in his favourite position on the toilet, overlooking the garden.

'It's a different house now. We can remarket it for the spring buying season.'

'I don't want to sell it now.'

'What!'

I took pity on his shocked expression.

'No, no. Don't worry, I'm not serious. You'll earn your commission all right. It's just that now that the alterations are complete, it's not such an effort and an inconvenience for me to visit it. It would be nice to enjoy it for a little bit before we sell it.'

'You'll have plenty of time to do that. You're going to have to do something about the garden. It's looking very neglected.'

He revised the sale particulars for the house, incorporating the changes which had been made and from April onwards, I started work on the garden. Now that I did not have to co-ordinate a team of workers, I based myself at home and travelled down to Fulford Mill for two days a week.

I dug over the heavy soil beside the septic tank and collected two trailer loads of mushroom compost from Baddow Mushroom farm and dug it in to break down the clay. A 40-foot tulip tree had stood in this spot and every spring its magnolia-shaped flowers had formed a soft pink canopy over the front garden until it had expired of rot and had fallen across our alsation Liz's grave.

I visited the Wyevale Garden Centre in Crossing to buy vinca for Roger's nine-inch gap between the kerbing of the forecourt and the retaining wall of the septic tank, but settled on lavender instead, continuing the line with a purple flowering, French rosemary beside the new fence and down to the mill pool. They had a tulip tree sapling in stock. I bought it and planted it close to the rotted stump of its predecessor.

I planted a *Viburnum Burkwoodii* underneath the dining-room window, to fill in beside the fence where the old carriageway had exited on to the lane and to echo the one in the front lawn, confident that it would grow into an exuberant bush, whose size could be determined by the next owner. I planted vinca and hypericum to spread down the river bank and fill in between the rosemary and the forecourt and to give foreground colour to the view of the mill pool.

Bob Hudson and his friend spent one entire weekend clearing it of dead branches, waterlogged tree trunks and the plastic bottles and containers which had been swept down the river over the years and had probably not been cleared since Bearman died in 1976 or I had made a half-hearted attempt, during one of my weekend visits in the intervening years. It looked lovely, with a robust, four-foot hemlock growing in the centre of the small island. Roger and I stood on the decking of the septic tank on a cold, April afternoon, composing a design of indigenous water plants, which would restore its former appearance and mentally positioned water forget-me-nots, marsh marigolds, arrowheads, water mace, brooklime and loosestrife.

The growing season had started in earnest and the garden sprouted alarmingly. The few hours which Brian could give to the garden each week permitted him to do little more than mow the lawns and trim the edges. The hedges grew at a prodigious rate in response to the alternating rain and sun and every spare moment that I had was spent trimming and pruning.

In the wash house, I found my mother's red, plastic, kidney-shaped kneeler that she used to put on the paths to protect her knees when she weeded the long borders. I took it out and started weeding the rose border down to the terrace. When had I last done that? It must have been in 1977, during my divorce from Nova. My mother and I had attacked it one Sunday afternoon, while my father slept in a dilapidated, striped deckchair in the shade of the fir tree, unable to decipher the print of the *Sunday Telegraph*. Unusually, she had been in a reflective mood.

'We haven't done this together for a good few years.' She smiled, as we filled the wheelbarrow with bindweed, nettles, ground elder and ragwort.

'You always enjoyed gardening didn't you?'

'You have to, if you live at Fulford Mill.'

'Did you do a lot of gardening when you were a girl?'

'No, I was born during the First World War and Daddy was invalided home at the end of it with Spanish influenza. The doctors told him he needed to live in a different climate. So he went off with my mother to run a farm in Nova Scotia. I was sent to grandfather Gaskain's house at Grove Park in South London, when I was three. I was eight or nine when they came back and then I was sent off to boarding school. Denis Gaskain gave my father a job, managing one of his farms near Petersfield, but there were gardeners and farm workers and anyway young ladies didn't do gardening in those days. But anyway you know all this, Savage.' Savage was her nickname for me, what its provenance was I had no idea.

'They were strange and excitable times between the wars when I was growing up, very different from today. Lots of servants, but transport was always difficult if you lived in the country and girls weren't expected to do anything except become wives and mothers. I was living on the farm at Froxfield when I met your father at a ball in London. He was very adventurous. He always seemed to be able to get hold of transport of one sort or another. He'd just started practising as a barrister and he didn't have much money, so he was managing the chemist's shop in Sloane Square on a part-time basis and living in the flat above the shop. We lived there for a short while after we got married and before we moved to York Gardens.'

'Why did you decide to live in Banktree?'

'It was cheap and your father was beginning to get a fair amount of work on the Eastern Circuit. That meant being in court in Chelmsford and Romford and Southend and Colchester.'

'He didn't seem very adventurous when we were young.'

'He was too busy. He wasn't just starting out then, he was getting on with it. Once he'd become established the work never stopped. He didn't have time to be adventurous.'

'He went through a very argumentative stage.'

'It was just words. Mind you, it irritated me at times too, but he was reliable and honest and wanted the best for you all. He never objected to paying for anything for the family he could afford. If you remember he never spent money on himself. He's had that old jacket he's wearing for 35 years. I bought it with him in Chelmsford, with the proceeds of a planning appeal which he had won. Anyway life's a trade-off isn't it, you take the good with the bad.'

'You never seemed very close,' I ventured. Was I going too far? Would she be offended by my impertinence? But she was in a pensive mood and I was interested in hearing her reply.

'Not while you children were young. We had too much on our hands with this place, but after you lot had left home we became much closer. It was quite like the old days.'

'Wouldn't you have liked to have had an outside job then?'

'In a way I would have, because I think I became a bit narrow-minded as I got older, but I was never very adventurous and by the time you'd all gone, I didn't want anything more demanding than the Citizens Advice Bureau. Besides, I knew you would be adventurous enough for all of us. I knew your life would be eventful. You were independent from the age of two, when you broke your arm trying to escape through the fence into the field.'

'It's been a bit up and down,' I mused.

'I knew it would be.' She leaned forward, favouring her bad hip as she unravelled some bindweed, growing up the yellow rose bush in front of her. She turned to look at me from her bending position.

'It'll all be the same in a hundred years,' she had smiled.

May was warm and June was hot. I began to worry about the survival of the new plants and bought a hozelock hosereel from B&Q, which I could fit to the springwater at the tap in the woodshed in order to water them. It came in a self-assembly kit in a sealed plastic bag, within a brightly coloured box.

I laid all the pieces out on the courtyard wall and examined the pictorial assembly instructions. On the back, in the twelve different languages of the Common Market, were abbreviated, written instructions, simplified for international cretins.

They were far too advanced for me. On the diagram, the pieces for each side looked the same, but looking at the pieces on the wall, I could see, with the aid of Roger's glasses, that in reality each one was subtly different, with fractionally larger or longer grooves into which the lugs from the opposing side should fit. The outlines on the printed diagram, however, were so thick that it was impossible to differentiate one piece from another. The permutations were endless.

I returned to the written instructions. Skipping through Portuguese, Italian and Spanish. I read the first line of the English: 'Lug A to Groove B. Rotate. Lug B to Groove A. Rotate Press.' There was no way to determine which was Lug A or Lug B. I read on. The last line was ominous: 'Warning! Once assembled the drum cannot be dismantled.'

I imagined the next owner of Fulford Mill inheriting a permanently lopsided hose drum. It seemed singularly appropriate. Millitis was as constantly mutating as a virus. Taking my courage and the two sides of the drum in both hands, I fitted lugs into grooves, rotated and pressed. It was with mixed feelings that I surveyed the perfectly cylindrical result. Still, the hypericum was saved.

The warmer weather brought not only the usual growth of bindweed and ragwort but also a new crop of would-be house buyers. The revived marketing campaign had resulted in a steady dribble of viewers, anxious to make their next purchase before the recovering economy signalled another housing boom, leaving them high and dry with their ideal home disappearing over the horizon, out of their price range. By the middle of June, David Forrest had received a number of inquiries and was particularly struck by a Mr and Mrs Cuthbert.

'I just think you'll like them, Charles. They have a very Fulford outlook on life.'

'You mean they like clutter, spiders, an overgrown garden and humping coal up from the cellar?'

'Yes.'

'Have they made an offer?'

'It's not quite what we're looking for, but they may go up a bit and I think you'd be pleased to sell to them.'

'I'd like to meet them,' I said, surprised at my own remark. I'd never wanted to meet the purchasers of the houses I'd modernized in London. 'Would that be all right?' I added, not wanting him to feel that I doubted his perspicacity.

'Of course, I'll send them over.'

They arrived on the first of July and parked by the septic tank. I stood on the front steps as a nice-looking couple in their late forties, early fifties walked slowly across the gravel, looking appreciatively down the riverbank towards the mill pool and taking deep breaths of the still, summer air.

There were none of the first moments of suspicion, when the vendor thinks, 'Who are these outsiders who are going to steal my property for less than its worth, criticize the decor behind my back and change everything with their new-fangled ideas?'

and the purchaser thinks, 'I bet he hasn't had any other offers and won't tell us that the boiler is on its last legs.' It was Steve and Margaret from the first handshake. Steve with a full head of hair, turned prematurely white from 39 years with Ford of Basildon and Margaret with a quiet, Sagittarian enthusiasm and a calm manner, reminiscent of my mother's more whimsical Cancerian variety. I made coffee and we sat on the patio in the July sun.

'I apologize for asking to meet you,' I said. 'It seems a bit impertinent, but this is rather an unusual place and I just wanted to be sure that the people who bought it knew what they were letting themselves in for.'

'Not at all,' Steve replied, 'we don't think it's impertinent. We appreciate you taking the time.'

'I just love it,' said Margaret.

I embarked on an explanation of the boundaries, the layout, the history of the estate, the neighbours, the ergonomics of the house, the alterations I had made and the things I had purposely left untouched.

'We know we will have work to do,' said Steve, 'but we think we can handle it. We have a few acres at home now and I've got an old 1960s Fordson tractor. I'm used to doing things around the place. It's my hobby.'

'I just love it,' said Margaret.

'What do you have in mind for the land?'

'I want to rear some cattle and I'd like to keep pigs as well,' Margaret replied.

My parents had lived through wartime rationing when even the essentials of life were scarce and I remembered myself walking up over the fields to Nutleam Stores in the early fifties with the rationbook of brown coupons for the weekly supply of sugar, but the land at Fulford Mill was good, rich Essex soil and provided an opportunity to augment the shortages of the postwar years, which was taken enthusiastically by my mother. Throughout the forties and fifties she had run Fulford Mill like a smallholding and when I was old enough to accompany her, we would go to Banktree cattle market in March or April and buy ten or twelve young bullocks to fatten up as stores in the pasture meadows and two or three litters of piglets to raise in the spare stables, which were not being used for horses.

I would insist on being the family bidder, as I stood on the middle rung of the wooden fencing pen surrounding the auction ring, as the market men in their long, brown coats prodded and poked the livestock around the enclosed space, while the auctioneer, with a brown trilby set jauntily on the back of his head, ran through their qualities, their pedigree and their breeding points. The sellers were all local farmers and the buyers were local breeders, rearers, slaughter-house men and butchers, so his recitation meant something to the ruddy-faced unshaven men who thronged the market in the old square on Wednesday mornings. Everyone knew the sound heart and lungs of Albert Fuller's Herefordshire bull and how his offspring were stayers which put on weight steadily. If David Sutton was selling a heifer from his Friesian herd, it was more likely because he had run out of milking capacity than because it was faulty and the bidding would be stronger than it would be for a single heifer from an outside herd.

The bustle, the noise of the men chattering and the cattle lowing, the pungent, agricultural smell of the livestock, mixing with the Woodbine cigarettes and the yeasty aroma of warm beer, were intoxicating to me. I gripped the top rail of the fencing, waving my livestock sheet frantically, as I bid with a jealous and proprietorial air for the lot which my mother had earmarked for Fulford Mill on Geoffrey Ratcliff's advice and the auctioneer acknowledged my excited bidding with a flick of his clipboard, as he rattled up the bids in a soft Essex burr with a Craven A jiggling in the corner of his mouth.

The pigs were my greatest delight. In those days, pig-rearing was not dominated by the Landrace and Large White as it is today, so that modern pigs are uniformly long, lean and white. The advent of the supermarket has brought with it a prejudice against colour and the modern obsession with healthy eating and its rejection of animal fat has meant that most pork sold today is pale, lean and tasteless. In the fifties, however, pigs were often black or spotted, with a regional identification and an individual character, quality and flavour and we would buy Essex Saddlebacks, Large Blacks, Gloucester Old Spots and even Tamworths. Each one had its own qualities and its own individual flavour and their meat tasted like real pork and bacon. But fat was their downfall. Having a greater capacity for storing fat than the Landrace or the Large White and their meat being of a darker and less uniform hue, these pigs have fallen out of favour to such an extent that many of them are now classified as rare breeds and the pork we buy in supermarkets today tastes like cardboard.

We kept a small flock of Rhode Island Red chickens in the stable yard, which would flutter on to the wall and fly down into the garden, to peck for worms and insects among the cabbages during the day and our breakfast soldiers would be dipped into big, brown eggs with bright, yellow yolks.

We had a sleepy-eyed, Jersey milking cow, called Rosie, who would be led out each morning into the willow plantation, to browse in the luxuriant pasture. I would ride her back down the lane, holding her leather halter, in the evening, for milking and we would churn her rich, creamy milk into butter in the dairy, tapping it into shape with the corrugated, wooden butter pats.

In those days, the large garden which I had cut in half to meet the conveniences of today, was in full production under Bearman's steady hand. Mr Lay's roast beef was accompanied by our own roast potatoes, parsnips, onions and bright green Brussels sprouts in winter or crisp runner beans in summer. The succulent pork from our own pigs was embellished by Lucy's apple sauce made from the tart Bramleys or the mellower James Greave cooking apples from the orchard and her crusty pies of rhubarb and gooseberry were augmented with raspberries and strawberries from the top garden. The slatted apple rack in the wash house was filled with firm, red Coxes and Blenheim Orange eating apples from the trees by the stable yard door.

And then there were the asparagus. On the other side of the path in front of the potting shed was an ancient asparagus bed and in late May, Bearman would begin to cut the pencil-thin, eight-inch shoots with his bone-handled pocket-knife. Lucy would cook them in boiling water on the Aga until they were *al dente* and we would sit at the square kitchen table guzzling them with melted butter, brown bread and Maldon salt, too engrossed to speak. They tasted like angels on my tongue.

I noticed that we always seemed to have more visitors during the asparagus season than at any other time of year and in April and May, when the growing season was in full swing, my mother and I would spend long hours in the late afternoon on hands and knees, carefully unravelling the long, creeping roots of the couch grass from the crowns.

'How old is this bed?' I asked her one evening as we filled the wooden trug with the straggling weed.

'I don't know. Nancy says she remembers it from when she was a girl, so it must be at least 60 years old.'

Since my departure and her death there had been no one to spend the time, kneeling in the compacted manure, and the couch grass had slowly encroached over the entire bed, strangling the asparagus in an act of horticultural sabotage on behalf of the growers of the pale and insipid imports from California.

'Do you have a family?' I asked the Cuthberts nosily, thinking that they would need someone to fill the bedrooms.

'Yes, two grown-up girls in their twenties and a boy of 14, John. Both the girls like riding, Lyn especially.'

'Well, the stable yard will be useful for you then.'

'Yes, and the paddocks. There is something for all of us here and we would enjoy it, that is the key. I just love it.'

They really were perfect purchasers. David Forrest had done it again.

'Charlie, it's Auntie Joan,' the brusque voice announced down the telephone. 'I'm on a pilgrimage. I want to come and visit your mother's grave on the 13th, the anniversary of her death. At my age I'd better come soon or I'll never make it. Can you put me up?'

Auntie Joan was my mother's cousin. They had grown up as neighbours, when my mother was living with her grandparents in Grove Park between the wars and had remained friends throughout their lives. She lived in Lymington now and her husband Mike had died four years earlier. Every year, she and my mother had gone on short breaks together, to the Lake District or the West Country, to escape from their families and be girls again together and she had been an ally of my own. She had lived in Hastings when I was at Summer Fields and I was sometimes allowed to walk down through St Leonards and have lunch with them on Sunday.

'Yes, of course. I'll drive down and pick you up.'

'No, no. Just pick me up at 12.05 from Witham station on the thirteenth. See you then.' The phone went dead.

I picked her up at the station on the thirteenth. She came striding purposefully out of the station, carrying an overnight bag. Now 78, the years seemed hardly to have touched her athletic bearing and peremptory air. A thin, agile woman, her dark hair mixed with grey, but the same blunt manner and the same lively look in her eye. She opened the car's back door before I could get to it and flung her case on the seat.

'Ah, my chauffeur, good.'

I went to give her a greeting kiss, but she waved me away as she got into the front seat.

'Don't waste time on that. Let's get to a pub.'

I drove to the Willows in Crossing and we ordered a Ploughman's each.

'Would you like a gin and tonic?'

'Gin and tonic! I'll have a beer.'

'What a half of lager or something?'

'No, a pint of bitter, dear boy. Good heavens, Charlie, where have you been! Still I suppose smart ladies in Surrey drink gin and tonics. I suppose Annette's a G and T girl.'

'Well she likes different drinks, pastis and . . .'

'Sensible girl, but it's a pint of bitter for me. Now then what I want to do is tidy up your mother's grave. I bet you haven't looked after it.'

'Well, Anne and Peter came over last year and they weeded it and this . . .'

'Exactly, well you can help me. We'll get a couple of trowels and tidy it up and then we'll buy a rose to put on it. Now let's have the other half and then we can get going.'

'It wasn't a half.'

'Oh, don't be so pedantic.'

The second 'half' disappeared in the time it took me to pay the bill and I drove my delightful aunt down to Crossing church. We set about weeding the overgrown grave, while she chatted about my mother, their childhood together, my grandmother, the Gaskain family and her own life. I sat on the grave of Jessie Kemp (1820–1896), as she titivated the edges of my mother's grave.

'Do you want to be buried or cremated?' I asked.

'Yes, it's a difficult one, isn't it? The fashion now is to be cremated, so much simpler, none of this weeding. But to my way of thinking, it partly depends on what you think of those that come after.'

'How do you mean?'

'Well, look at us, sitting here chatting over your mother and her life and times, your sisters, your family and mine. It's part of family history isn't it and the only reason we're doing it is because your mother was buried. If she'd been cremated, I might have been saying a prayer for her in my local church, but I wouldn't have travelled up here and been chatting with you. If you're cremated, it's a bit impersonal to go to where the ashes were scattered and think, "Well, I think a bit of Rae was dispersed by the roots of that old beech tree underneath where the garden roller is now" or look at an urn and think, "Those look like the ashes from the Aga." '

'So how does your opinion of those that come after affect it?'

'Well, it's obvious. If you think they'd enjoy doing what we're doing now, then get buried and they'll have somewhere to come for a chat and pass on a bit of what you stood for.'

'And have a "half" at the pub.'

'Exactly. But if you think they're a bunch of nincompoops, then get cremated and let them get on with it.'

At the beginning of August, I received a courteous letter from

Steve and Margaret, explaining that they were going to have to pull out of the transaction. Their own purchasers had been dependent on money from a legacy in order to buy their house, but getting their hands on the money had proved harder than they had anticipated. I thought of my Great Uncle Walter and realized that it could be the next millennium before they were able to move.

The letter was written in a tone of great disappointment and I found I had mixed feelings. On the one hand David Forrest was right, I would have been happy to have sold to them. They were a lovely couple and they would have fitted well into the Fulford community. On the other, I had done so much work at the house and it had rekindled so many memories that I was developing a proprietorial air about it.

I decided to wait and see what happened. David Forrest continued to market the property, but it was the holiday season and most English people's minds were on buckets and spades and not on moving. I was summoned down at the end of August to meet a Chinese lady from Hong Kong who was interested, but I knew from experience that orientals and Fulford Mill were not an obvious match.

Sure enough, in the middle of September, the Cuthberts found another purchaser for their house and revived their offer. Once again I accepted it.

On 12 October, I drove down to meet them at the house, to discuss what items of the remaining fixtures and fittings they would like to buy and to see Richard Shaw to complete our replies to the list of inquiries for the sale.

It had been raining intermittently for three weeks and it was drizzling as I left Surrey. The rain increased as I hit the M25 and by the time I pulled off the A12 to take the back lanes from Hatfield Peverel, it was lashing the windscreen so hard that the wipers couldn't clear it. I pulled off the lane into the muddy gateway to a field of sugar beet and sat looking through the liquid windscreen across the flat, Terbing fields to the impressionist outline of Hazelton Wood, as I waited for the downpour to abate.

By the time I reached Fulford Mill, the rain had settled into a steady cascade, which drummed rhythmically on the roof of the car. I ran up the front steps into the house and stood, looking out through the living-room window, as the level of the river rose under the relentless deluge.

It rained solidly until two and then abruptly, as if a rat had got stuck in the pipe, the rain stopped and a thin, October sun melted through the watery-grey cloud cover. I put on my wellingtons and went outside. Roger had raised the sluice gate to it highest level and the water burst through the brick tunnel under the lane with the power of a fireman's hose, jetting in a brown, earth-laden explosion into the mill pool with a thunderous roar. Nonetheless the level of the mill leat was rising inexorably above the level of the lane, as the run-off from the fields of the valley swelled the torrent, which had accumulated in the upper reaches of the river. The pipe, which took the original course of the river under the lane at the bottom of the hill from Black Nutleam, was hopelessly inadequate to take the volume of water and a ford of eddyingy brown flooded the lane for a 100 yards, drowning the pedestrian bridge. In the centre of it, a blue van from Newmarket had been swept against the concrete stanchions of the bridge and the elderly driver looked forlornly out of his open window at the rising waters, as a charitable local, thigh deep in the swirling current, attempted to persuade him to abandon it. I waded in and together we pushed the car to safety, as the river reached the top of the leat and spilled down the safety channel through the willow plantation, swelling the ford and gushing down the natural river course.

I returned to the house and walked down through the dripping shrubbery. The tail water had risen to the top of its banks and flooded the nut walk. George's wooden footbridge was still in position, but it was floating at one end where the stays had rotted through and was perilously close to being swept away. A brown moorhen fluttered excitedly in its extended territory in the overhang of the hazel trees. The stream, which took the spring water opposite the cottage, had spilled over the lane and rushed down through the channel in the garden, cascading over the brick steps by the terrace, flooding the tennis court. An overfed magpie, the size of a young pheasant, stood on the bank, flicking its long, black tail feathers in irritation at the inundation of its favourite hunting ground and a sociable robin hopped inquisitively ahead of me into the shelter of the blue cedar.

I walked up past the giant oak between the fields and crossed the meadow to the elbow in the river. The valley, as far as Bluebell Wood, was impassable under two feet of drifting, grey water. I turned back along the hedge, watching four, prosperous rabbits scampering excitedly in the wet grass in Ossie Claricoat's field, telling me that it wasn't going to rain again today, as I filled the pockets of my anorak with firm, ripe field mushrooms.

Rain, in a town, is an inconvenience and a discomfort, making parking difficult and shopping impossible, as pedestrians dodge puddles and umbrellas, hustling from one shop awning to the next, trying to keep the rain off their necks and out of their shoes, as they buy the week's groceries. Rain at Fulford Mill though is weather to take notice of. Bulls had forded the river for eons in the low-lying fields which were impassable to blue vans and the Mill itself had been built to take advantage of the flow of water. The hamlet had thrived on water power for centuries and rain gave it an identity and purpose which was both a treat and a delight.

Next morning, Steve and Margaret arrived at 9.30. I wished they had been here yesterday. I knew they would have loved it.

We walked around the house, chatting like old friends, as Margaret commented, 'Yes, we'd like that. We'd like the carpets and curtains too, Oh that mirror would be useful. What about this chest, Charles, and the chandeliers? Yes, we'd like the wardrobes, we've got more bedrooms to furnish.' As she raised a questioning eyebrow over her shoulder to Steve who smiled resignedly, as husbands do, when their wallets are being plundered, but they have a happy wife and a good bargain. I was pleased too, that so many things, that had formed a part of my memory of Fulford Mill, were going to be of use to them in the future.

We stood in the doorway between Lucy's bedroom and my own.

'This is going to be Sharon's sitting room,' said Margaret. 'She sorts herself out well, doesn't she? She's going to have your bedroom, this is her en suite living-room and she's right next door to the bathroom.'

I was pleased that my old bedroom was going to such a perceptive girl, who appreciated the positioning of the new bathroom. I could imagine how she would redecorate the two adjoining bedrooms that Lucy and I had occupied and I could already hear the laughter of her friends as they sat in Lucy's room, looking out over the lane, chattering over this new chapter in her life.

We walked out to the stable yard and I pointed out the various items that I wanted to bequeath to them. The old saw-bench, the rest of my father's oak paling, a selection of garden implements, old but still serviceable, Rom's woven, canvas girths, the metal cornbins, the old chalk vat for lining the tennis court, a pig trough and an ancient upright bicycle with a leather seat, which had stood in the top garage from the first days of my memory and had been inherited by us from Francis Blyth.

'You may think this is rubbish and prefer that I remove it,' I said hesitantly, not yet certain of their definition of rubbish. 'But I think that they are all part of the character and history of Fulford Mill and you are very welcome to have them.'

'Oh no, we don't think they're rubbish,' said Margaret quickly, 'we'd love them.'

'I've got some blades that will fit the saw-bench,' said Steve, examining it with a practical eye.

We stood among the garden implements in the top stable.

'How do the haylofts run above us?' Steve asked.

'The run is divided by the walls of the second garage with its entrance from the lane,' I replied.

He climbed up the wall ladder and poked his head into the empty loft. 'Ah yes, I see. Goodness, it's enormous.'

'We'll lose John for days on end here,' Margaret smiled.

We walked back to the house and I made coffee, as we got out paper and pencils and began to make a list of the items they wanted and to scan my replies to their solicitor's inquiries.

'What are you doing with the cottage?' Margaret asked.

I explained the problem of the subsidence and the underpinning which would be necessary.

'Why do you ask?'

'Lynn has got her eyes on it. It's just a short walk across the paddock to the stables.'

Mentally, they'd moved in already.

Chapter Nine

In negotiating the sale of the house to Steve and Margaret it had been agreed between us that I would retain an extra sliver of land with the cottage and reduce the price of the house accordingly. They had been happy with the arrangement since they were already stretching their finances in taking on the house. I had felt that the extra piece of land would make the cottage more saleable and so it had proved.

David Forrest had received several offers to purchase the cottage from people attracted by its superb position. But they had all fallen through when their surveyors had identified the cost of the repair work that would be necessary to make it habitable and particularly the underpinning necessary to stabilize the subsidence from which it suffered. The extra-strip of land, however, had given it an additional benefit and shortly after Steve and Margaret revived their offer, we received a firm offer for it from Mr Knight. He worked for a house-building company and he had had a structural survey carried out and had spoken to the planning department of Banktree district council. He had obviously assessed the extent of the project which he would be taking on thoroughly and since he was also interested in buying one of the fields on the opposite side of the lane as a pony paddock, it seemed to me that he was a perfect purchaser for the cottage, somebody who was capable of capitalizing on its potential and who would fit in with the horse-loving Cuthberts.

I was concerned, however, that if Steve and Margaret eventually did not go through with the purchase of the house, another purchaser might see the loss of the sliver of land to the cottage as being a disadvantage. I did not want to proceed with Mr Knight until I had reassured myself that I would not be prejudicing the sale of the house to others.

I drove down in the morning of 17 October and after lunch of Bosnian stew, Roger's culinary *pièce de résistance*, the contents of which he thankfully kept secret from me, I walked up to the oak tree between the fields to review the line of stakes that marked the boundary of the land to be retained with the cottage. I turned and looked back to the house, and marvelled in the kaleidoscope of pastel colours that met my eyes. The advent of autumn had dispersed the urgent hues of summer and, at the corner of my right eye, the oak tree in front of the cottage sported a vivid canopy of orange, like the unruly hair of a ginger-headed schoolboy. Below it, the pale green of the stand of four lime trees which bordered the cottage garden led to the flaking blue and grey trunks of the eucalyptus trees, standing in the shadow of the massive copper beech, which stretched out its huge arms of variegated russet. Beside it, the delicate silver-grey needles of the blue cedar flickered in the light breeze, confident that the approaching winter would not harm them.

The white, weather-boarded gable of the top floor of the Mill peeped, with its single window, through the dark-green uniform of the giant redwood, which towered over the bay window of the house, like a lookout in the crow's nest of a schooner. In the corner of my left eye, the picture was framed by a long line of gentle greens and yellows and browns, waltzing carelessly on the hazel trees bordering the nut walk in their last dance of the season.

A pale, autumn sun flitted through the drifting clouds, casting alternate light and shade, constantly changing the subtle hues, like a child playing with the colour control on a television. It was like a living Constable and I wondered what it would be worth in auction.

On 20 October, David Forrest rang me. The Cuthberts' offer had become doubtful again. The purchasers of their house had had a structural survey done and wanted a reduction of £20,000 to cover the defects that had been uncovered.

'Would you be willing to reduce the price of Fulford Mill to help them go ahead?'

I thought about it. In many ways they were the perfect purchasers and I had grown to like them and would be saddened by their disappointment, but it was the same old catch 22 in the house-sale chain. My house needs £20,000 spent on it, and I can't go ahead with the purchase of your house unless you pay for it, or at least contribute to it.

Steve and Margaret had had a survey done on Fulford Mill and it too had thrown up various defects, hardly surprising in view of its age and maintenance record, but they were nothing like £20,000. Whereas I could see the fairness in making a contribution towards the cost of remedying the defects of Fulford Mill, I couldn't see the logic in contributing towards the cost of a house I'd never seen for the benefit of purchasers I didn't know.

Then again, once the defects of Fulford Mill were specified and costed, I might very well carry them out myself. It was three and a half years now since my father's death and I had already carried out a considerable number of alterations. One more wouldn't be a great hardship and there was no pressure on me to sell now. I could be selling at a time when the market was at a low ebb. I might get a better price next spring and my position as executor required me to get the best price for the property. It seemed to call for the judgement of Solomon, a role I felt singularly unqualified to fill.

On 23 October I received another courteous letter from Steve explaining all the circumstances. Between the lines I read not only disappointment at this most recent hurdle, but also a sense of trepidation at the size of the project they would be taking on at Fulford Mill. I had been convinced, in my own mind, that they would have found it immensely rewarding and I didn't want them to miss the opportunity through understandable second thoughts.

I sat down in my office and wrote a long, careful letter, explaining in detail the alterations which I had made to the house, the things which I had intentionally left unaltered and those items which I felt needed some attention for the purpose of good maintenance. I added a detailed section on optional alterations, which I would make if I were to live in Fulford Mill, in order to make sense of the kitchen, scullery and larder and to make the bathing arrangements more convenient at the front of the house.

It took me two hours and I sat looking at the six pages of A4 paper, surprised at my own industry. Why had I done that? I realized that the letter was only an expression of my own views, which may or may not have been of interest to them. They were intelligent people with ideas of their own. If they went ahead and bought the house, they would decorate it and alter it in their own style and I shouldn't burden them with my ideas. Besides, all my comments were irrelevant to their problem of the moment, which was money.

I decided to heed my mother's observation in her letter to my father in 1937 and tear it up. Instead I wrote a much shorter letter, offering either to do some of the remedial work at Fulford Mill myself, or alternatively to make a slight reduction in the price, to allow them to do it and at the same time to give them the carpets and curtains at no cost, to ease their overall financial burden. On 3 November, I received their reply:

Oak Lodge
Thorndon Park
Brentwood
Essex
2 November 1993

Dear Charles,

Thank you for your letter of 29th October.

I accept and understand your comments regarding the surveys and reports. We would certainly wish any repair and refurbishment programme which we carry out to be under our direct control, especially as we will have to live with the results!!

Your price reduction, therefore, is a much preferred option and, along with the offer on carpets and curtains, has provided sufficient room for manoeuvre for me to get a final agreement from our buyer.

I spoke with him last night and now have him reconfirmed with all the issues raised by the survey report put behind us.

I will advise my solicitor today of the appropriate adjustments and now look forward to an exchange of contracts.

Thank you for sharing your plans for the cottage with me and I appreciate your offer to keep me updated.

With kind regards,

Steve and Margaret

The next day I picked up the telephone to Richard Shaw: 'Yes, I've heard from the Cuthberts' solicitors and the sale is confirmed with the new terms. There is one thing, though, their purchaser is in the jewellery business and doesn't want to move during December, which is his busiest month. Can you complete and move out within November?'

'That only gives us three weeks. I'll have to speak to Roger.' I rang the house. Roger's answerphone was on. I panicked. I hadn't bothered with the process of completing the sifting of the clutter during the period when I had been carrying out the alterations and the house was still full of our possessions and Roger's. He would need plenty of notice to sort out space in the Mill and move his belongings. Was he away or just out? I left an urgent message on his machine and jumped into the car.

I stopped off at R J Shaw & Co in Banktree. Richard was out, but the sale contract was ready and I signed it, so that he would have it available for exchange. Glenys, his secretary, gave me a covering letter which he had written, explaining that if Roger and I couldn't organize clearing out the house within November, then completion would take place in January.

I drove on to the house. Roger was there and had received my message. We walked round the house together, considering the feasibility of moving out within the three weeks. We opened the door of the junk hole and my heart sank. It was still full of junk: wine racks, boxes, files, the wooden store cupboard, household paraphernalia from the fifties.

'Actually, we could move out quite easily,' Roger said.

'But there's still all this junk, here and in the wash house and dairy, the stables and garages.'

'Most of it's mine.'

'What, all this?'

'Yes. I've got a lot of the same junk as you. Besides many of the things you don't want, I might like.'

I looked at him with fresh eyes.

'Do you, by any chance, spend much time at Witham council tip?' I asked.

'Come on, let's get on with it,' he replied, picking up an empty cardboard box and beginning to fill it with electric irons, a thermos flask, a toaster and other kitchen utensils which would have dressed the set of the very first Oxo commercial in perfect period.

I went into the scullery, opened all the cupboards and put the crockery, pyrex dishes, saucepans, baking tins and cooking utensils on the floor. They covered it. I couldn't get back to the door. Was it really three and a half years since Juliet had said: 'We might even clear the house on this trip.'

Roger went up to the stable yard and collected some boxes which he had saved from his own move. He threw them to me across the carpet of period impedimenta and we spent the afternoon and evening packing up. At least, I did, while he leaned against the door with a cup of so-called tea, passing erudite comments on the age, provenance and future use of the items I was packing and gratefully accepting those for which I could see no future use. His pile grew rapidly.

'And this is a gift for Tabitha,' I said, passing him a blue saucer, which had lost its cup.

Talfryn had brought a metal detector down on his last visit and had combed the garden and the two front paddocks. He had found quite a collection of old nails, an ornamental handle for a cake stand, some modern coins and a Roman one. They stood on the shelf above the sink as I did the washing up from our makeshift supper.

'I expect you'll want these,' I said, pointing to the rusty pile of metal.

'Actually,' Roger replied, peering at the pile and sifting through it with his fingertips, 'I do want this.' He picked up a screw with a flat eye-head. 'I need one of these for the machinery of the millwheels and they are no longer available.'

He had been working intensely for some weeks on a series of films about cats, to be released on videotape. After supper we sat in the living-room and watched the final edited version. Much of the material had been filmed in the garden and fields at Fulford Mill and in the Mill building itself, using Tabitha and Leroy as models.

One of the tapes was entitled *The Mystery of the Cat*, and gave an exposition on their prominence as fertility deities in ancient Egypt 3,500 years ago, through to the belief in England in the 1580s that they were the servants of the devil. Roger interrupted the tape.

'You realize that we are in the heart of witch-finding country.'

'No.'

'Oh yes, Matthew Hopkin, the Witchfinder General lived in Manningtree. The pub still exists where he held his sessions. In fact, one of the most celebrated cases of alleged witchcraft took place in Hatfield Peverel. The pamphlets about it still exist. A Mother Waterhouse and her neighbour and the neighbour's daughter were accused of being in league with the devil. The cause was that she owned a black and white spotted cat, with the unfortunate name for the defence, of Satan. During her ownership of the cat, her neighbour's cattle got the blight and her husband died. She gave the cat to her neighbour and the neighbour's husband died. So the neighbour gave it to her daughter and the daughter's baby died.'

'So what happened?'

'They were tried for witchcraft by the attorney-general himself and hanged. Another notorious case occurred at St Osyth, where 18 women were hanged for being a coven of witches, one of them because she put wool in a basket for her kittens and was thereby considered to be giving comfort to the devil.'

He touched further on the demise of the Knights Templar, accused by Philip the Fair of worshipping cats and it seemed curiously appropriate that the Mill, which had once formed part of their estates, should have reverted to another worshipper of cats, or was this some satanic plot? I would have to take care in offering comfort to Tabitha in future.

'Rog, do you think I could have that blue saucer back?'

Late in the evening, we went over to the Mill and sat in his enormous open-plan kitchen among the massive oak beams.

'I love this smell,' I said.

'Yes, it's the wood and the dust. I was lucky that it was so dry. Many mills of this period have rotted and collapsed, because when they became redundant, their owners stopped spending money on maintaining the roof. Your father did very well to keep this one weathertight.'

'He always used to complain about the cost.'

'I'm sure he did, but he did well. This was a very sophisticated mill for its period. For example the hoist which was used to draw the sacks up to the cornbins on the top floor has a clutch system. The wooden wheel on the top floor, which the chains wrapped round when it drew the sacks up through the building, was constantly turning. But it has a loose belt, which can be tightened by pulling on a rope which ran through these ropeholes from the top of the Mill to the bottom. When the man on the ground floor had tied his sack on to the chain, he could pull the rope, the belt would tighten and the pressure on the chain would ease in, instead of being sudden, so the sacks wouldn't leap off the ground and split.'

'Wasn't that normal?'

'No, usually he would have to lift the sack himself and ease it up using his muscles.'

'Were there any other refinements in this mill?'

'Yes, look at this.'

We walked over to a large metal piece of machinery enclosed in a solid cover, about the size of a work bench.

'This is a roller mill. They became popular in the 1890s when tastes were moving away from the heavy puddings of the Victorian era to lighter pastries and puddings at the turn of the century and people started wanting white flour instead of stone ground. This machine could strip the husks off the corn so that it gave white flour, but it was then fed down to the mill stones on the floor below. So this mill was producing white flour but still using its old stones.'

The kitchen was on the second floor, which had formed the engine room of the Mill and the drive shafts, which ran off the vertical shaft rising from the turbine on the ground floor, were each lined with metal wheels.

'They certainly used the water power in a lot of different ways.'

'Yes, this second shaft takes the power up to the top floor to turn the wheel, which lifted the sacks. The wheels on the first shaft were used for a variety of different purposes. The first one ran the generator so that you had your own electricity. That is quite recent. I should say that was installed in the 1930s.'

'Yes, we used to generate our own electricity in the house up until I was a teenager. We always knew when Bearman was knocking off work, because the lights would dim when he switched from direct current to battery. That changed when we went on to the mains.'

'That was in 1959.'

'How do you know?'

'Because when the electricians rewired the house, they found various pieces of newspaper in part of the old electrical installation, which were dated 1959. This second wheel was used to drive the knife-grinding stone, the third one to power the roller mill and this very large one fed down into the floor below, where the mill stones are.'

'What was that for?'

'I'm not absolutely certain, but I think it was an extractor fan.

The wheel on the lower floor is much smaller and therefore because of the gearing effect, whatever machine it was driving must have been turning very rapidly. Mills were prone to explosions, because flour in suspension in air is highly combustible. Since whatever machine it was was situated on the floor which contains the stones, I imagine that it must have been an extractor mechanism to suck the suspended flour out through the window.'

'It's interesting to hear how the place worked.'

'Didn't your father or yourself ever go into its background and use?'

'Not really. We had some background information about it, through Bearman and Dick Weller and local farmers and as I said, we generated our own electricity from it, but otherwise it was just the biggest conversation piece on earth. Douglas Hale and I made part of our first film in it.'

'What was that?'

'It was in 1960. It was a 20-minute film called *John*. In those days before videotape, or even the customary use of colour, film-making was very expensive and therefore a difficult hobby for a student. *John* was filmed in 16-millimetre black and white. It was a self-indulgent story about growing up in those times. It was an idea I'd had when I was at school.'

'How did you get the money to make it?'

'It took months of scrounging off friends and family and doing holiday jobs. The London School of Film Technique loaned us the equipment and one of the staff gave his services as cameraman. The sound track was principally folk music and a Scottish folk singer called Alex Campbell performed for us for nothing.'

'What happened to it?'

'It was shown in the Edinburgh Film Festival that year in the young film-makers section. A week before the festival, Douglas rang me in a panic saying that they needed an advertising poster for the film. I remembered a long-haired graphic designer called Dave who used to sit with us sometimes drinking coffee in the Troubadour in the Old Brompton Road in London. He knocked up an excellent poster in 20 minutes flat and we sent it off to the festival.'

'This must have all been very exciting. Was it the beginning of your film career?'

'In a way. We were convinced that the film was a masterpiece. Hollywood beckoned. The week of the screening arrived. All the critics were there. Next day we bought all the newspapers and scoured the arts pages for the reviews. The only one I can remember said "*John*, a production by teenage film-makers featuring the music of Alex Campbell, but principally identified by its highly imaginative advertising poster." I think it was more the beginning of Dave's career than mine.'

We went down to the ground floor of the Mill and Roger pointed to a pile of heavy oak beams.

'If you can come down next week and help me move these beams to their position over the mill race, I could use the space to store my furniture and anything of yours that you haven't decided the future of.'

Next morning I filled the boot, back seat, foot-wells and parcel shelf of my car with books, before driving back to Surrey. I had to brake suddenly at the Dartford Crossing when a green Vauxhall intruded into my lane and the books cascaded around my ears. I got out to sort out the mess and the grey-haired toll-keeper came out of his booth to help me. He perused the titles of the books as he handed them to me in the back seat, passing erudite comments on Jane Austen and Robert Browning. Finally he held out a mud-spattered copy of the *Inner Temple Yearbook* of 1984.

'Could I buy this off you?' he asked hesitantly.

I looked with astonishment at the budding legal archivist. Was it going to be this easy to dispose of the books?

'Please accept it as a gift,' I replied.

'Well, thank you very much.' He smiled, lifting the arm of the toll-gate and ushering me through, waiving the 90p toll (No change given).

Back home in Surrey I unloaded more than 500 volumes into my office and revelled in the ownership of the 1947 edition of

Good Poultry Keeping by C E Fermor and Frederick Litchfield's learned 1906 volume *How to Collect Old Furniture*, a subject on which I clearly need no outside advice, having collected a great deal by simply opening the garage doors at Fulford Mill. Unfortunately, there was no appendix giving an explanation of what to do with the old furniture, once acquired.

Halsbury's *Laws of England*, *The All England Law Reports* and the rest of my father's legal books I earmarked for Talfryn. He would probably be needing them from one side of the dock or the other. The *Shorter Oxford Dictionary* still contained no definition of 'sprigget'.

Among the books, I found my mother's autograph book from her schooldays at Tortington Park in Arundel. It was full, not only of the neat, ink signatures of schoolgirls who would by now be in their late eighties if they were still alive, but also little aphorisms, poems and homilies. I was particularly struck by Phyllis Dennis's offering of 13 April 1923:

> Jim came to teach her arithmetic
> He said it was his mission,
> He kissed her once, he kissed her twice
> And said, 'Now that's addition.'
> But as he added one to one
> In silent satisfaction,
> She timidly gave him one back
> And said, 'Now that's subtraction!'
> But Pa appeared upon the scene
> Quite angry with derision.
> He kicked poor Jim three streets away
> And said, 'That's long division.'

None of the books seemed to have any value, being mostly dog-eared and falling apart at the bindings, until I came to a beautiful leather-bound version of *Pilgrim's Progress*. I looked at the fly-sheet with interest. It had been printed and published by Brightly & Childs in 1817. I flicked through the thick pages of vellum and it seemed to be in almost perfect condition; a collector's piece, it must have a considerable value, a real family heirloom. I wondered which of my ancestors had acquired this edition, which had obviously been looked after with great care for over 170 years. I turned to the front inside cover and learned that it was the property of Thomas West.

On Monday I drove down after lunch to help Roger and Simon move the oak beams. I arrived at 3.30 and went in by the lane door. The office was empty. Simon suddenly appeared in the passage from the hallway.

'Hello, Charles, how are you?'

'What happened? The office is empty.'

'Yes, we moved Roger's furniture over to the Mill on Friday, and those bits of yours.'

'What about the wood?'

'We got that finished in the morning and Roger decided to keep going.'

I wandered through the house. It was virtually empty and unbelievably cold. Bare of furniture it seemed enormous. I dropped my suitcase in the living-room and walked up the lane to check the cottage. The lane was full of men from the Highways Department, digging out the stream and installing concrete kerbstones on the corner, where a lorry had knocked down the fence and hedge at the top of the garden. Mr Harris, the supervisor, was young and nervous.

'Are you the owner?' he asked.

'Yes.'

'Oh good. I need to see everyone. It seems we're in a bit of trouble. I was told to start clearing out this ditch, I mean stream. I'm not allowed to call it a ditch. I started this morning and the owner of the farmhouse rang the office and said he was going to take out an injunction to stop the work. It seems that stream bed belongs to him. Do you know anything about it?'

'I'm afraid not.'

'Do you know anything about the stream or ditch on the other side of his gate, opposite your corner? I've got to clear that out too?'

'I'm afraid not. It doesn't belong to me. I shouldn't think it belongs to Mr Russell either. He lives in that house behind the hedge, but it would be a good idea to clear it because it floods the corner after heavy rain.'

'Yes, I know. That's why I've been told to clear it, but I don't want to get into any more trouble.'

'I don't think the Russells will object. Their garden floods after rain because the spring water comes down the hill there.'

'Who owns the spring?'

'That's an interesting legal question. The spring comes to the surface in the field behind mine on the other side of the railway line. A number of people have an interest, but who owns it is a different matter. Does a spring belong to the person whose land it surfaces on, the people who use it or the statutory undertakings, who have the right of management? The Russells, Fulford Mill House and Fulford Cottage have a prescriptive right to draw water from it. The spring itself is on the land of a farmer who doesn't use it. It flows underneath the railway, so British Rail presumably maintain the culvert but the National Rivers Authority have overall management of all national water. I should ask Michael Beaver,' I added vengefully.

'Oh well, thanks for your help. I've got a meeting with the owner of the farmhouse now. I've got to smooth a few ruffled feathers. Do you know him?'

'No, he's only been here a few months.'

At that moment the owner came out of the front door of the farmhouse.

'Hello, I'm Andrew Parker. Are you from the Highways?'

'No, I'm from the Mill house,' I said, introducing myself.

'This is Mr Harris from Highways, but I'm pleased to have met you at last.'

I left them arguing the difference between streams and ditches and proceeded to the cottage. It seemed secure and unvandalized. I went back to the Mill, as Roger arrived from having taken some aerial photographs of the Mill with Al Gosling, a friend of Talfryn's whose father Martin, another alumnus of St Margaret's had been a footballing friend of my own.

'Ah Charles. Good, how's the sale going?'

'Fine so far, but I was going to give you a hand with the wood.'

'Yes, we've gone on a bit since then. I've moved my stuff and your bits, but there is one problem. We've run out of oil.'

'So that's why the house is so cold.'

'Yes, but you can have a bath. I've put the immersion heater on and we can light a fire in the living-room.'

'What about food?'

'Well we could get an Indian.'

'I'd prefer a Chinese.'

'That's what I meant. Have you had pneumonia?'

'Yes, why?'

'Well, I suggest you move your bed into the living-room and make up the fire.'

He took Simon home and collected an Indo-Chinese, while I made up the fire in the living-room and humped my bed down to the one warm room in the house. We sat eating the Indo-Chinese on the floor in front of the fire, off the small oak table that I had bought with the £5 that Lucy had given me on the occasion of my marriage to Nova.

'God, it's cold,' he said, as Liz rang from a warm hotel room on location in Ross on Wye.

'Yes, I think I'll shut some doors,' I replied, getting up.

'Don't do that!' Roger shrieked, interrupting his conversation with Liz. 'We'll never get out. You can't open that door from the inside.'

He finished his conversation with Liz and grinned at me. 'I think we've come full circle with this house. First I got drenched by the burst pipe in the scullery on the day I moved in. When we'd fixed the immediate repairs, I moved my belongings in. Then you carried out all your alterations. Now I'm moving out and you're moving the rest of your stuff into the Mill. On the day I move out the oil runs out and we nearly get locked in the living-room. Does this merry-go-round ever end?'

'No, it's called Millitis.'

He left for his adult education lecture and I went up to Lucy's bedroom to empty the bits and pieces from the drawers of the chest, which I was bequeathing to Steve and Margaret. In the top drawer, I found a letter to my mother from her father, dated 22 August 97, but I think he meant 79, lamenting the move from their home at Birling Gap into the nursing home at Bexhill, which had been forced on them by old age and incapacity. The letter was concerned principally with his worries about storing their furniture. In the end, it had been stored at Fulford Mill and mentally I ran through an inventory of its present whereabouts for his benefit.

The letter started with the one word 'Adorable' and ended 'Better luck to you all, darling and our best love, Daddy.' The words seemed to convey all the poignancy of their lives; of what might have been, if liquidation, poverty, war wounds, mustard gas and Spanish influenza had not fractured their world. In another life would his business have prospered, would they have had more children, would my mother not have been farmed out to her grandparents and developed the protective shell of self-sufficiency that became a central part of her personality?

Christmas was coming and in the big, empty house I could hear the laughter of bygone Christmases, when my grand-parents had stayed with us and time had healed some of their wounds. My grandmother making a nuisance of herself in the kitchen and getting under Lucy's feet, as she put the crockery back in the wrong place because she wanted to be helpful. My grandfather standing with his back to the fire in his regimental tie and cavalry twill trousers or smiling benignly, as he let me win at chess. They were happy Christmases for the lonely Warrenses and I thought what a catalyst my father had been for them all, with his argumentative ways and good intentions and realized at the same time that he would never get any credit for it, except perhaps from me.

Next morning, I loaded up my car with the last of the books, the sporting prints from the passage and the *Cries of London* from the living-room. Roger brought a cup of coffee over from the Mill, as I folded my bedding into a plastic bin-liner. The phone rang. It was Richard Shaw.

'Ah, Charles. I've exchanged contracts, but the Cuthberts' purchaser can't move before the end of the month, so completion is fixed for 14 January.'

I put the phone down.

'That's it, Rog. We've exchanged. They're moving in on the 14 January.'

'So we needn't have rushed after all. I could have had a relaxed Christmas in the house, entertaining all my relatives. On second thoughts perhaps it's just as well. Life goes on, for all of us doesn't it.'

'It does.'

He helped me load up the car.

'Will you be coming down again?'

'I'm not sure. It's pretty much finished now, isn't it. Perhaps one last visit for old time's sake.'

'I hope so. It would be nice to see you again, but if not there'll always be a spare bed in the Mill, if you're passing this way in the future.'

'I'd like that.'

We shook hands, smiling awkwardly as men do, when they have formed a friendship and don't know how to express it. I got into the car and turned on the smart, gravelled forecourt. I drove slowly out of the new gate and up the rise to Black Nutleam. In the rear-view mirror, Roger pulled the gate shut behind me. I waved out of the open window, as I disappeared round the curve in the lane, before the ford, but he was closing the latch of the gate and didn't see my farewell.

Over Christmas I has the uneasy feeling at the back of my mind that there were still bits of clutter left in the house. I hadn't really done a proper clearance when I'd packed up my bedding. I hadn't checked through all the cupboards, or the upstairs bedrooms. I didn't mind leaving to Steve and Margaret items that could be classified as memorabilia, but I didn't want them to start their own adventure surrounded by our rubbish.

New Year's Day fell on a Sunday, so Monday was a Bank Holiday. The property market was picking up and my desk was covered with projects for appraisal. January was going to be busy. If I wanted to check the house one last time before it passed out of our ownership, then Monday looked like being the only opportunity.

It was raining as I turned off the A12 at Kelvedon and meandered through Silver End and Crossing, letting the memories of another time drift through my mind. The rainwater permeated my worn-out shoes as I walked through the long grass of the pretty graveyard of Crossing church and paid a soggy au revoir to my parents and to Lucy as they lay at peace in the shadow of the three misshapen Douglas firs.

Inside the house I filled no less than nine plastic bin-liners with the remaining rubbish and left them outside the house for the accommodating dustmen of Banktree district council. I checked through every room in the big, cold house. That was it. Apart from the items which I was leaving for Steve and Margaret the place was empty. We had moved out.

I went outside and walked through the garden for the last time, breathing the air deeply. Was the air at Milton Abbas any better? The Cuthberts had spent the week between Christmas and the New Year moving some of their belongings into the stables. Steve had bought a job lot of 72 railway sleepers, no doubt as part of some master plan for the future. They stood, piled neatly against the wall of the stable yard. It reminded me of my father's pile of oak paling and I smiled as I wondered if they would still be in the same position in 47 years' time, a new mutation of Millitis. I found it exciting that I didn't know what they were for and that somebody else's ideas and energy were going to take Fulford forward into the next century.

I wandered slowly back to the house, as Roger and Liz appeared from the Mill.

'I thought we'd got rid of you,' Roger grinned.

'It's not as easy as that.'

'Well, come and share our lunch,' Liz smiled.

We went up to the second-floor kitchen and I picked up a metal spar from the dresser.

'What's this, Rog?'

'It's the damsel. Do you remember when those boys broke in. They told the police they'd thrown it down into the hole where the mill wheel used to be. Well, Simon retrieved it. It's the key part of the mechanism to move the grinding stones. Now all I need is a sprigget, but you can't get them anywhere. People don't even seem to know what a sprigget is any more.'

He looked at me, as if he was confident that I would share his amazement at this ignorance.

'I think I know where you could get one,' I smiled.

An Appendix

Aspects of The Mill's Life
by Roger Tabor

The Landscape and Watermill's Marsh

Fulford Mill as it stands today is mainly Georgian, like the main section of the Mill house alongside it. Yet parts of both buildings are centuries older and stand in a landscape that was constructed for the Mill and its buildings much earlier, probably in Saxon times. Few realize that the landscape is an integral part of the machinery of the Mill, and here the wildlife-rich marshland and river channels have remained unchanged for centuries.

The watermill was once the sole source of machine power in the village and manor. Driven by the river, it underwent many changes over the centuries, from grinding corn and treating cloth – by fulling, from which it gets its name – to producing electricity. After decades of retirement it has become a house, while being restored as a mill.

The marsh upstream of the Mill was used to control water levels and prevent flooding, but it also provides a genuine wetland haven for wildlife in a surrounding landscape that has become increasingly hostile through drainage. The Mill's marsh both straddles the millhead stream and also envelopes both sides of the old river. It is an ancient landscape, for in addition to the plants of the marsh the bank that runs along the millhead is host to dog's mercury, an indicator of very old woodland. The far side of the marsh is bounded by a medieval ditch and bank which has massive old oaks and is dotted with bluebells and more dog's mercury.

All through this century the marsh has featured a crop of willow trees that are grown especially to make cricket bats. In part of the marsh in the summers of his youth, Charles and his sisters used to graze their ponies.

The Mill's marsh is one of the last few still managed in a traditional way which keeps a wide range of summer wild flowers surrounded by hosts of butterflies. In high summer it is a delight of pink and white flowers of codlins and cream (the old country name for great willowherb) which drift as far as the eye can see, interspersed with the frothy white meadowsweet. This was Queen Elizabeth I's favourite flower and it was strewn throughout her palaces, just as it was on the floors of the sixteenth-century part of the Mill house, to give a wonderful vanilla scent overlaid with a certain sharp tang.

Everywhere are small tortoiseshell, red admiral, peacock butterflies whose caterpillars feed on the abundant nettles that thrive on the fertile silt from the river. Comma butterfly caterpillars live on the hops that grow wild in the marsh, and skipper butterflies dance about the yellow vetchling flowers.

A managed working landscape, but of such antiquity that it is a relic of the river valley from before the Mill was built many centuries ago. As a wildlife habitat, it is unsurpassed.

High Waters of the Mill

The sluice controls the amount of water that passes through the Mill relative to the amount that crashes down a weir into the splash pool.

The Mill owes its very existence to the river, and the sluices and channels were made to harness the power of the water. Across the one third of a mile from the end of the marsh to the Mill the original river falls by fifteen feet. By building the mill-head channel or leat direct to the Mill, and building the bank along its length to hold back the water, the early buildings kept the water at the same height all the way to the Mill where it could all cascade at once. It is this height of water at the Mill that turned the wheel. Many mill leats throughout Britain were dug in Saxon days, and nearly all of them by the fourteenth century.

The sluice itself is a very old structure. As it stands it is made of late eighteenth-century brick, but work by the Environment Agency investigating a leak found that inside it is an earlier wooden sluice built probably in 1707. The brick part had just been built round it.

Behind the Mill is an enormous stand of butterbur, a huge leaved plant that grows mainly behind watermills because it doesn't like the disturbance of agriculture, and there was always a quiet spot by a watermill. The butterbur like the stands of iris and water figwort is only there because the high water level has been kept for centuries by the Mill's sluice.

The Mill is now a relic of a bygone age. Yet at one time nearly every village with a river had a mill, and the lushness of this river vegetation has been maintained by the Mill, along with enough water to navigate upstream. When children, Charles and his sisters boated upstream of the Mill in the strange triangular craft they had part made, part salvaged from the sluice with 'Bunny' Bearman, the Mill house gardener and sluice controller.

The depth above the Mill has also given good conditions for a range of damselflies as dragonflies to thrive in. I love to paddle upstream in high summer and banded demoiselle damselflies flutter all around. Resident kingfishers dive for fish to feed their young in the millhead pool. However, like many rivers in Britain the water could be better, but it does support mayfly nymphs and freshwater shrimps.

The very siting of the Mill and Mill house is probably due to small freshwater chalky springs that run down the valley to the buildings, for in centuries past the cloth industry mills often washed foul materials into the river. The Mill's sluice, by keeping the river up to work the Mill in the summer, preserved the habitat and stopped the river drying out. In winter, the river is 'flashy', rises quickly, and the miller had to watch his sluice control. However, as the river rose it would tip into the marsh from the millhead and old river which delayed the rise and protected the buildings. On moving to the Mill I legally became a miller, and had to very quickly learn the intricacies of sluice control! The ancient design of the Mill's landscape reduced the risk of winter flooding, yet stopped the river disappearing in the summer. The old system is still working and is a classic example of what could happen again nationally.

The Working Life of the Mill

At every generation in the Mill's history changes have been made to the building as its function changed - as with many mills in Britain. The appearance of the outside of the Mill today relates directly to its working life through the nineteenth century as a most productive flour mill. At its peak it operated 6 sets of millstones, three pairs of which still remain in place today. It had a waggon and a two-wheeled cart, with a stable of heavy horses beside the Mill house, where Charles and his sisters kept their horses this century.

The waggons would bring the grain to below the Mill's lucom (the part of the Mill that projects from the top of the building). The hoist chain, powered by the water, would take the sacks of corn to the top of the Mill. The Mill stopped grinding in 1947 when bought by Charles' father, but the hoist still regularly worked for storing grain until 1959.

I am particularly fond of the hoist as it is worked by the oldest wooden piece of machinery in the Mill, a large wooden wheel that drives the chain drum. Its axle can be raised or lowered by the miller pulling a rope that was both geared and counterbalanced. This changed whether the drive belt from the water was slack or taut, and amazingly acted as a clutch on wooden machinery. The hoist could operate outside or through an internal series of 2 inch thick elm board trapdoors. These were so balanced as to be self closing. Automation in wooden machinery!

As the grain entered the Mill it was weighed, and again as it left as flour, but the total honesty of millers in giving fair measure throughout the ages has been often doubted! The grain was stored in huge bins in the floor below the lucom stage. It then travelled by gravity down wooden shutes down to the stones that still stand as they were left by the last miller, Mr Weller, as he downed tools when the Judge bought the Mill. One set lie open to be dressed by hand, to cut a new working face. Another is in full readiness for work, with its tun that kept the flour in, and the wooden 'horse' whose four-legged frame kept the hopper bringing the grain to the eye of the stones. At its heart is the 'damsel' that acted as a 'cam-shaft' acting against a willow spring and shook the grain down the slope of the 'shoe', and so affected how much grain entered the stones for grinding.

During the nineteenth century the new arrival of grain from the prairies of USA and Canada was disastrous for country mills, for brand new mills were put up at the docks using the newest technology of roller mills. In roller mills, the distance between the rollers could be accurately set, and so whip off the husk and produce white flour. Fulford Mill competed by adding a small roller mill which they worked in conjunction with the stones.

A steam engine was added so the original three water powered stones could be joined by three steam powered sets of stones. The new big mills were linked into the new Victorian railway system to reach towns throughout Britain, and most country mills lost the competition. But this mill had its own railway siding built on the nearby line and, with a shuttle service using its own waggons, was still in the fight. In 1893 its final solution was to take out its water wheel and put in a turbine. Although there are no written records of the size of the waterwheel, it was over eight feet wide from the channel width, and by measuring its gouge on the tunnel wall I found it to have been a nineteen foot diameter wheel. Despite that huge size the turbine, which is really a vertically operating water wheel that worked under a head of water, could produce 50 per cent more energy from the same amount of water. These changes bought the Mill a much longer life but, like most remaining country mills it became an animal feeds mill by the First World War.

These changes were just overlaid on earlier ones. For most of its life the Mill was both a fulling and corn mill combined. The fulling stocks for beating cloth were in line on the ground floor, until they were removed in 1813 when the industry died in East Anglia.

Times Past

The manor was once owned by King Harold, before the Battle of Hastings, and at the Norman invasion it went to Count Eustace of Boulogne, then to Queen Matilda, and then to the Knights Templar. They were warrior monks who ran their estates to pay for their fighting and castles in the Holy Land, and had considerable numbers of sheep. The flat east of England was probably the main wool and cloth production area in Britain.

Following the disgrace of the Templars, the Knights Hospitallers became the beneficiaries until the dissolution of the monasteries. During this long ecclesiastical period the Mill would have been worked for both treating cloth by fulling and grinding grain.

At the Dissolution in 1541 the Mill, Mill house and surrounding land went into private ownership. The oldest part of the Mill house is a timber framed building with wattle and daub infilling that dates from around this period. In 1656 was described as 'Fhullford Mill ffarme a house well built with barnes, stables, with Corne and Fhulling Mill'. The manor was then bought by a group of adventurers, who intended to split up the estate and sell it in bits.

In 1669 there is a record which notes: 'Fulford Mill with a handsome house, a fulling mill and a corne mill, most the house and mill new built'. This coincides with the doubling in size of the Mill house by building an upper floor, again timber framed.

In 1679 a document witnessed by John Evelyn shows the Mill and Mill house sold off by the widow of one of the adventurers, but they were bought back by the new owner of the estate. However, by the early eighteenth century, the Mill was fully independent, and in 1707 a new owner, William Draper, funded major works on both buildings. Remarkably most of the crafts-men's invoices from this rebuild survive. There are notes from the millwright, carpenter, suppliers of bricks, nails and so on. They reveal that a new set of millstones cost the then large sum of £11.10.0. The timber framed Mill house had 'underpinning' of a new brick plinth.

The new owner rented the Mill out to the miller Daniel Wade for an annual amount of £63. Wade agreed to 'keep in good and sufficient repair the said Mill, Millhouse and all things belonging to the said Mill, Millhouse, dwelling house, barns and stables, and all gates, stiles, hedges and ditches, and shall not copp or topp any tree not hereto for lopp'd or topped, - nor grub up any'. He also agreed 'to keep scoured and cleaned yearly all banks by the foresaid mill stream or waters pursuing from the said mill'. The tradition of coppicing certain trees around the Mill and Mill house continues to this day.

During the eighteenth century the fulling was central to the economy of the Mill and it was probably around 1780 that the main part of the Mill house and Mill in its present form were built. There is less documentary evidence of this building work, but the building itself can be read. The bricks of the Mill are hand-made and some of them have diagonal folds on them, typ-ical of the way bricks were handled during drying in the late eighteenth century brickyards. In the rebuild of the Mill, much of the fabric of the earlier mill was incorporated. There are won-derful old elm floorboards. The new materials included massive beams thirteen metres long, 37 cm (15 inches) square.

However, the cloth industry was in decline, and the fulling stocks stopped working when the last fulling owner, Joseph

Saville, sold the mill to Richard Dixon in 1813 and from then on it was just for grain.

During the late nineteenth century individual workers like the young Dick Weller wrote their names inside some of the huge corn bins after they had finished the backbreaking task of clearing one out.

Changing Times

Nancy Blyth, who was brought up in the Mill house during the last period of active working life of the Mill as an animal feeds mill, recalls with affection hearing the tap, tap, tap of Mr Weller, the last miller, dressing the stones. During the ownership of the Blyths, beans and oil cake were crushed in new machines. Only smaller amounts of grain needed storage in the bins and the new products did not need to go through the whole mill. Consequently a pair of new double doors were put in half way up the Mill for more direct access using a wooden ramp as well as the hoist chain.

The story of the Mill is the story of grain-milling and the cloth industry through a millennium across many parts of Britain. Yet within that individual lives have been led, everyone with separate stories. The common feature that has linked the lives of those that peopled this book are a pair of special buildings - the Mill and Mill house.

After a long working life the Mill stood empty, as did the Granary alongside and the millhouse's cottage. When the judge died the Mill house also stood empty. All over Britain obsolete agricultural buildings lay crumbling for years, some never to recover. Many watermills did not survive this century, having lasted for many centuries before.

Now at Fulford the turbine has been freed after silting up for many years and water is again passing properly through the Mill. There is a clatter of horses hooves once again back in the Mill house stable yard, and all of the buildings have new people bringing a new phase to their buildings' lives.

Yet the Mill's life and that of the Mill house and Granary could have been very different but for Charles Llewellyn's concerned care. It is not something he would say himself, yet as you have walked with him through the pages of this book, relishing his humour, you will have found his affection for the place in which he was brought up shines through. I am grateful to him for writing down the story, for reading it has brought me many smiles as I think back, for somehow I had become part of that story.

Roger Tabor 1997